Notebook on Shipwrecks

Maryland
Delaware
Coast

H. Richard Moale

HERITAGE BOOKS
2007

HERITAGE BOOKS
AN IMPRINT OF HERITAGE BOOKS, INC.

Books, CDs, and more—Worldwide

For our listing of thousands of titles see our website
at
www.HeritageBooks.com

Published 2007 by
HERITAGE BOOKS, INC.
Publishing Division
65 East Main Street
Westminster, Maryland 21157-5026

Copyright © 1990 H. Richard Moale

All rights reserved. No part of this book may be reproduced or transmitted in any form or by any means, electronic or mechanical, including photocopying, recording or by any information storage and retrieval system without written permission from the author, except for the inclusion of brief quotations in a review.

International Standard Book Number: 978-1-58549-178-0

ACKNOWLEDGEMENTS

To list all who have helped in making this book possible would be a volume in itself.

I do wish to thank especially Captain Robert Byre who started me into this research by sharing local lore and his vast knowledge of the wrecks off Delaware and taking me to visit those sites over the years. Captains Ed Brex, Bill Tattersall and John Steffey of Ocean City, Md, also contributed information about the wrecks while aboard their boats; my friends and I would dive into the deep, cold water exploring the final resting place of many proud ships plying the waters off Maryland and Delaware.

The Mariners Museum of Newport News, Va, provided the bulk of the photographs contained herein, and hours of research in their fine library yielded other data about many of the ships. Nathan Lipfert of the Maine Maritime Museum in Bath, Me, really filled in much information about a lot of the wrecks as a surprising number of ships had their beginnings in Maine's shipyards.

Early diving buddies Manny Pospisil, Bob Barbarite, Sue Sepelak, and Jim Prow helped collect "on site" data by snooping in and about each wreck looking for clues to its identity. Not being trained archeologists, we sometimes took the difficult route to discover what remains we were visiting, especially without the use of the modern sophisticated equipment available now.

My wife, Lorraine, deserves much credit for her patience and understanding while I buried myself in books, microfilms, and news articles for countless hours at various libraries in Maryland, Delaware, and Virginia also waiting on shore for the time I spent offshore diving these mysteries of our maritime past.

For the many hours of typing, editing and putting all of this information into readable form, I thank Linda Meijer who gave of her time and talent to make the book a reality.

FORWARD

This book represents an attempt to list, by alphabetical order, shipwrecks along the coast of Maryland and Delaware from Cape Henlopen at the Northern limit to Maryland-Virginia line at the Southern limit to a distance of approximately 40 miles offshore. The listing includes all sinkings occurring between 1664 and 1975 regardless of tonnage. I have taken care to present only data of record, but caution the reader or fellow researcher who uses this book, that not all information about the wrecks listed here is proven fact, nor is this a complete list of all sinkings. Wherever possible, on site data has been collected over a period of twenty years about wrecks that can be documented and explored by divers. The incomplete data for the ships listed in this book challenges those who come after me to complete this study and perhaps add more names to those wrecks of mysterious origin lying within the coast waters of Maryland and Delaware.

Editor's Note: The newspaper articles in this book were copied as they were written.

Alphabetical Index
(By Ships Name)

Name	Rig	Date Sunk	Page
ADDIE	Schooner	November 7, 1902	8
ADDIE TODD	Brigantine	March 8, 1884	9
ADELINE	-	December 9, 1824	10
ADELINE TOWNSEND	Schooner	January 12, 1909	11
AFRICAN QUEEN	Tanker	December 29, 1958	12
AGNES MANNING	Schooner	November 20, 1889	16
ALFRED	Brigantine	January 21, 1882	18
ALLIE H. BELDEN	Schooner	March, 1888	19
ANNA & ELLA BENTON	Schooner	September 10, 1889	19
ANNA MURRAY	Schooner	February 17, 1902	20
ANNAPOLIS	Brigantine	October 1, 1774	20
ANNIE E. GALLUP	Steamer	February 21, 1918	21
ANNIE T. RULAND	Sloop	October 20, 1904	21
ARIEL	Brigantine	August 20, 1785	21
ATLANTIC	Schooner	August 9, 1843	22
AUSTERLITZ	-	January 12, 1828	22
BALTIMORE	Ship	November 29, 1753	22
BARNEGAT	Barge	March 31, 1942	23
BAYLIES WOOD	Schooner	April 3, 1887	25
BEAULIEU	-	August 30, 1802	25
BERTHA	Ship	December 31, 1886	26
BETSEY RICHARDS	Schooner	September 13, 1843	27
B.F. MACOMBER	Oil Screw	July 20, 1946	28
BOSTON (H.M.S.)	-	March 1, 1695	30
BRAVE (H.M.S.)	-	April 12, 1806	30
BRINKBURN (S.S.)	Steamer/Screw Schooner	1887-1888	30
BUENA VISTA	Brigantine	October 31, 1853	31
CADET	Schooner	February 9, 1842	31
CALINARCHER	Yacht	December 3, 1942	32
CANCEAUX	-	1772	32
CANTON BRITON	-	January 1, 1867	33
CARPENDER	Schooner-Barge	December 12, 1933	33
CARRIE E. BUCKMAN	Schooner	April 6, 1889	34
CARRIGAN	Schooner	March 29, 1903	34
CASPIAN	Oil Screw	March 16, 1953	35
CASEY & BROWN	Oil Screw	November, 1975	36
CASTEL	Brigantine	June 23, 1841	36
C.B. HAZELTINE	Ship	March 12, 1888	37
CELESTE	Schooner	January 10, 1903	38
C.F. SARGENT (U.S.S.)	Barge	July 31, 1918	38

Alphabetical Index
(By Ships Name)

Name	Rig	Date Sunk	Page
CHAMPION	Sidewheeler	November 8, 1879	39
CHARLES P. SINNICKSON	Schooner	September 17, 1876	50
CHARLES P. STICKNEY	Schooner	September 10, 1889	50
CHARLOTTE	Brigantine	November 15, 1853	51
CHATTAHOOCHEE	Brigantine	December 18, 1846	51
CHEROKEE (U.S.S.) #458	Tug	February 26, 1918	52
CITY OF GEORGETOWN	Schooner	February 2, 1913	56
CITY OF ORLEANS	Schooner-Barge	November 14, 1923	60
CLEOPATRA	Steam Screw	October 29, 1889	65
COMMERCE	Merchantman	1771	69
CORNELIA	Merchantman	1757	69
CREW LEVICK No. 5	Barge	April 11, 1923	70
CRICKET	Barge	September 28, 1890	70
CRYSTAL WAVE	Sidewheeler	October 29, 1889	71
DAUPHIN	Brig	March, 1744	73
DAVID H. ATWATER	Steam Screw	April 2, 1942	73
DeBRAAK (H.M.S.)	Sloop of War	May 23, 1798	75
D. & E. KELLEY	Schooner	December 21, 1887	77
DEERHOUND	Schooner	March 5, 1769	80
DETERMINEE	Brigantine	March 26, 1803	80
DORA	Schooner	October 1, 1915	81
E. BUCKMAN	Schooner	February 21, 1842	81
ELECTRIC SPARK	Steam Screw	July 10, 1864	82
ELIZA ANN HOOPER	Schooner	September 10, 1889	83
ELIZABETH	Ship	February, 1702	83
ELIZABETH	Schooner	December 18, 1846	84
ELIZABETH DeHART	Schooner	July 5, 1888	84
ELIZABETH PALMER	Schooner	January 26, 1915	85
ELLA	Schooner	November 25, 1888	89
EMILY A. FOOTE	Oil Screw	August 23, 1930	89
EMILIE E. BIRDSALL	Schooner	February 4, 1908	90
ENOCH TURLEY	Pilot Boat	November 30, 1843	91
EQUATOR	Steam Screw	March 23, 1893	92
ESTHER ANN	Schooner	October 9, 1920	93
EUSTATIA	Ship	1664	94
FAITHFUL STEWARD (H.M.S.)	Ship	September 2, 1785	94
FORRESTER	Brigantine	September 16, 1843	96
FORTUNE	Brig	November 29, 1764	96
FRANCIS BURRETT	Schooner	November 21, 1879	97
GARLAND	Ship	April, 1709	100

Alphabetical Index
(By Ships Name)

Name	Rig	Date Sunk	Page
GENERAL BERRY	Bark	July 10, 1864	100
GENERAL MIFFLIN	Brig	March, 1777	101
GEORGE H. BENT	Schooner	December 18, 1888	102
GEORGE L. GARLICK	Sloop	November 25, 1889	103
GEORGE G. SIMPSON	Steamtug	March 14, 1888	104
GOOD HOPE	Ship	October, 1670	104
GORDON C. COOKE	Barge	April 22, 1947	105
GOVERNOR JACKSON	Schooner-Barge	August 22, 1888	107
GREYHOUND	Man-of-War	August, 1750	108
GUERNSEY	Snow	September 13, 1734	109
GYPSUM PRINCE	Steam Screw	March 4, 1942	110
HANNAH A. LENNEN	Steam Screw	June 16, 1944	113
HAPPY RETURN	Snow	October 1, 1747	113
HARRISBURG	Schooner	September 13, 1846	114
HARRY K. FOOKS	Oil Screw	September 10, 1941	114
HENRY & CHARLES	Ship	1796	115
HERCULES	Barge	January 19, 1901	115
HESPER	Gas Screw	April 30, 1919	115
HVSOLEF	Steam Screw	March 11, 1942	116
IL SALVATORE	Brig	-	118
IRA D. STURGIS	Schooner	February 15, 1906	118
JACOB JONES (U.S.S.)	Destroyer	February 28, 1942	119
JAMES R. MARKS	Sloop	September 10, 1846	129
J. HENRY EDMONDS	Gas Screw	March 13, 1928	129
JAMES DUFFELD	Schooner	April 30, 1912	130
JAN MELCHERS	Ship	May 2, 1888	130
J.D. ROBINSON	Schooner	September 10, 1889	131
JOHN	Ship	1797	131
JOHN J. WARD	Schooner	March 5, 1907	132
JOHN McMAKIN	Sternwheel Steamer	August, 1860	132
JOHN PROCTOR	Schooner	September 13, 1909	133
JOHN R. WILLIAMS	Steam Screw	June 24, 1942	134
JOHN SHAY	Schooner	September 19, 1901	136
JOHN W. HALL	Schooner	March 12, 1912	137
JONESPORT	Barge	February 18, 1937	138
JOSEPH E. HOOPER	Schooner-Barge	November 15, 1945	139
JUANITA	Barge	February 17, 1902	140
JUNIPER	-	1861	141
JUNO	Warship	October 29, 1802	141
KITTY	Snow	May 22, 1764	142

Alphabetical Index
(By Ships Name)

Name	Rig	Date Sunk	Page
LACEDEMONIENNE	Brig	January 1, 1799	142
LACEDAEMONIAN	-	July 12, 1798	142
LENAPE	Steam Screw	November 18, 1925	143
LEIV ERICKSON	Schooner	September 1, 1910	145
LEWIS CLARK	Steamer	September 6, 1888	146
LIZZIE CRAWFORD	Steamtug	March 14, 1888	146
LIZZIE THOMPSON	Schooner	April 16, 1883	147
L.S. LEVERING	Schooner	February 23, 1901	148
LUCY E. FRIEND	Schooner	November 14, 1910	148
LUCY NEFF	Steam Screw	December 15, 1915	149
LUTHER A. ROBY	Schooner	October 11, 1896	152
MAGDALEN (H.M.S.)	-	1780	152
MAID OF THE MIST	Gas Screw	September 24, 1920	152
MAJOR WILLIAM H. TANTUM	Schooner	September 10, 1889	153
MANHATTAN	Steam Screw	November 20, 1889	154
MARATHON	Brig	October 3, 1795	157
MARIA JOHANNA	-	March 10, 1784	157
MARIE C. BEAZLEY	Schooner-Barge	February 8, 1927	158
MARIE F. CUMMINS	Schooner	November 14, 1908	159
MARION CHAPPELL	Schooner-Barge	October 10, 1925	160
MARION O'BOYLE	Barge	November 12, 1923	161
MARLBOROUGH (H.M.S.)	Man-of-War	November 29, 1762	163
MARQUIS de SEIGNELAY	-	August 22, 1788	163
MARY & LOUISE	Snow	September 17, 1739	163
MARY ROGERS	Schooner	January 20, 1892	164
MASCOTTE	Bark	February 12, 1888	164
MATTIE W. ATWOOD	Schooner	December 18, 1887	165
MERMAID	-	1781	165
MERRIMAC	Schooner	April 10, 1918	166
MIMA A. REED	Schooner	September 10, 1889	167
MINNIE & GUSSIE	Schooner	January 30, 1891	168
MONTGOMERY	Steam Screw	January 7, 1877	168
MOONSTONE	Yacht	October 15, 1943	169
MORO CASTLE	Bark	November 25, 1888	171
MOUNTAINEER	Steam Packet	June 26, 1850	171
NANCY JANE	Brig	January 16, 1846	172
NELFRED	Oil Screw	October 15, 1956	173
N.B. MORRIS	Bark	February 28, 1902	173
NEOSHO	Schooner	August 18, 1919	174
NETTIE R. WILLING	Schooner	April, 1903	174

Alphabetical Index
(By Ships Name)

Name	Rig	Date Sunk	Page
NEW ORLEANS	Steam Screw	October 11, 1917	175
NINA (U.S.S.)	Steam Screw	February 6, 1910	177
NORENA	Schooner	September 10, 1889	179
NORTHERN PACIFIC	Steam Screw	February 8, 1922	180
NORTHERN 35	Schooner-Barge	February 14, 1927	182
NORUMBEGA	Schooner	April 23, 1906	183
NUMBER SIX	Schooner-Barge	April 3, 1915	184
NUMBER NINE	Schooner-Barge	April 3, 1915	185
NUMBER ELEVEN	Schooner	February 28, 1906	186
OAKDENE	Steam Screw	March 2, 1895	187
O.C. CLEARY	Brig	November 12, 1883	188
OCEAN BIRD	-	January 2, 1799	189
OCEANUS	Schooner	September 28, 1890	189
O.D. WITHERELL	Schooner	April 21, 1911	190
OLIVE BRANCH	Brig	September 10, 1846	191
PASSIAC	Schooner-Barge	May 27, 1922	192
PATRIOT	Bark	May 23, 1889	192
PATTIE MORRISETTE	Barge	January 24, 1935	193
PATUXENT	Schooner	December 19, 1846	194
PHANTOM	Steam Yacht	April 9, 1904	194
POSEIDON	Steam Screw	July 31, 1918	195
POWHATTAN	Oil Screw	April 10, 1961	196
PORPOIS	Brigantine	September 22, 1855	196
POSTILLON	Schooner	February 2, 1803	196
PRINCESS ANN	Ship	February 2, 1698	197
PRINCESS CAROLINE	Ship	April, 1903	197
PRINCIPESSA MARGHARTA de PIEMONTE	Bark	March 12, 1891	197
P. TEE	Oil Screw	May 27, 1970	198
PYLADES	-	December 3, 1810	199
QUANGO	Brig	February 3, 1880	200
QUATTRO	Bark	February 17, 1887	201
RACEHORSE	-	November 15, 1777	201
RAPIDAN	Steam Yacht	September 10, 1901	202
RED WING	Schooner	October 23, 1891	202
RETURN	Sloop	September 9, 1787	203
RETRIBUTION	Ship	1839	203
RIVERDALE	Schooner	March 30, 1884	203
R.F. LOPER	Brig	December 16, 1841	204
SAETIA	Steam Screw	November 9, 1918	204
SALAS	Brigantine	November, 1881	208

Alphabetical Index
(By Ships Name)

Name	Rig	Date Sunk	Page
ST. EUSTATIA	-	December 30, 1783	210
SALLIE W. KAY	Schooner	January 10, 1883	210
SALVATORE	Barge	September 10, 1889	211
SAMARANG	Schooner	1826	211
SAN GIL	Steam Screw	February 4, 1942	212
SAN LORENZA de ESCORIAL	Ship	September, 1820	213
SAN MIGUEL	-	October 3, 1795	213
SAN VICENZO FLIORENGO	-	December 27, 1818	214
SANTA ROSALEA	Merchantman	1788	214
SANTO CRISTO	-	-	214
SANTO LEOCADIA	Ship	1828	214
SARAH W. LAWRENCE	Schooner	February 10, 1909	215
SARAH C. PARK	Schooner	September 10, 1889	217
SCORPION	Brigantine	July, 1759	217
SCULLY	Schooner	March 30, 1919	218
SEA BIRD	Schooner	September 16, 1903	218
S.G. WILDER	Schooner-Barge	July 3, 1933	219
SINGLETON PALMER	Schooner	November 6, 1921	220
SOLON	Brigantine	November 9, 1846	222
SOUTHERN SWORD	Steam Screw	March 18, 1946	223
STARLIGHT	Schooner	August 2, 1901	225
STRICKLAND	Snow	December 16, 1754	225
S-5 (U.S.S.)	Submarine	September 1, 1920	226
SUNBURY	Schooner-Barge	August 17, 1910	235
SUNRISE	Barge	April 6, 1889	236
SUTTON (S.S.)	Screw-Schooner	January 20, 1900	238
TALBOT	Schooner-Barge	October 28, 1938	240
TECUMSEH	Schooner	March 2, 1892	241
TENA A. COTTON	Schooner	February 4, 1907	242
THADDEUS	Schooner	May 19, 1846	242
THOMAS TRACY	Steam Screw	September 14, 1944	243
THREE BROTHERS	Ship	August 16, 1775	245
TIMOUR	Ship	September 10, 1889	245
T.J. HOOPER	Schooner-Barge	January 23, 1935	246
T. MORRIS PEROT	Schooner	September 28, 1913	247
TWO BROTHERS	Schooner	October 22, 1845	247
URANUS	Steam Packet	May 10, 1887	248
VESTAS	Tug	-	248
WALTER	Ship	October 21, 1844	249
WASHINGTONIAN	Steam Screw	January 26, 1915	250

Alphabetical Index
(By Ships Name)

Name	Rig	Date Sunk	Page
WESTERN BELLE	Schooner-Barge	September 23, 1917	254
WHITE BAND	Schooner-Barge	January 24, 1908	256
WILLIAM G. BARTLETT	Schooner	March 12, 1888	256
WILLIAM H. DAVIDSON	Schooner	March 26, 1903	257
WILLIAM ELLISON	Schooner	September 10, 1902	258
WILLIAM HALES	Bark	November 8, 1895	259
WILLIAM R. GRACE	Ship	September 10, 1889	261
WILLIAM H. SMITH	Schooner	January 30, 1903	263
WILLIAM O. SNOW	Schooner	September 12, 1889	264
ZELINDA	Bark	July 10, 1864	265

NAME: ADDIE

RIG: Small Schooner

REGISTERED NUMBER: 106183

DATE & LOCATION BUILT: 1883; Wilmington, Delaware

DATE SUNK: November 7, 1902

REPORTED POSITION WHERE SUNK: 1-1/4 mile south and 1/2 mile east of Indian River Inlet Station (U.S.L.S.S. record)

MASTER AT TIME OF SINKING: Captain Lathberry

CARGO: lime

HOME PORT: Wilmington, Delaware

LAST PORT OF CALL: Salem, New Jersey

PORT BOUND FOR: Millville, Delaware

CONSTRUCTION: 16 tons gross; 15 tons net length 41.5'; breadth 15.7'; depth 4.2'

OTHER DATA: All 3 persons aboard were saved.

NAME: ADDIE TODD

RIG: Brigantine

REGISTERED NUMBER: unknown

DATE & LOCATION BUILT: 1873; Calais, Maine

DATE SUNK: March 8, 1884; collision with a Steamer, City of San Antonio

REPORTED POSITION WHERE SUNK: 10 miles off the Delaware Lightship

OWNER: Boardman Brothers

MASTER AT TIME OF SINKING: Captain Crowley and 6 men aboard

CARGO: sugar and molasses

HOME PORT: Calais, Maine

LAST PORT OF CALL: Manzanilla, Cuba

PORT BOUND FOR: New York

WEATHER CONDITIONS AT TIME OF SINKING: dense fog

CONSTRUCTION: 233 tons

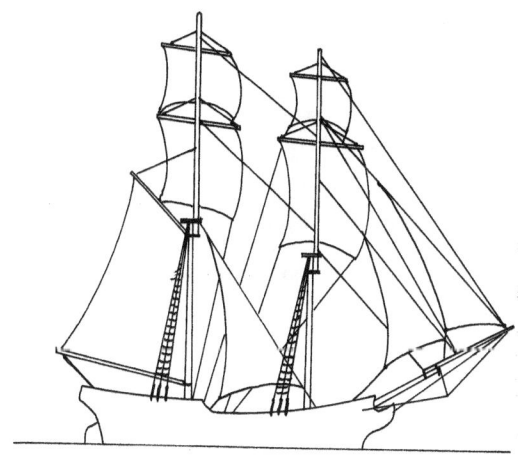

Brigantine

OTHER DATA:

New York Times, March 19, 1884
RUN DOWN BY A STEAMER.
THE BRIGANTINE ADDIE TODD SUNK DURING A DENSE FOG

The steam-ship City of San Antonio, of the Mallory Line, which arrived yesterday from Fernandina, brought the crew of the brigantine ADDIE TODD, which she ran down and sunk off the Delaware Light-ship during her outward passage. The collision occurred at 8 a.m. on March 8 during a dense fog. The steam-ship was proceeding cautiously and sounding her fog whistles at regular intervals. Captain Crowley, of the lost vessel, said that he did not hear the whistle of the steam-ship until she was close upon him. It was then too late to avoid her. A large hole was stove in the port bow of the schooner, between the bowsprit and the cathead. The hole extended below the water-mark, and the brigantine began to fill as soon as the two vessels had drifted apart. The crew of the brigantine hurriedly launched their boat and got into it, saving only a portion of their effects. They had barely got away from the wreck before she began to sink. Within 30 minutes after the collision the TODD had disappeared.

The steam-ship sustained no injuries of a serious nature, and she proceeded after having taken on board the brigantine's crew, which consisted of the Captain and six men. Captain Wilder, of the City of San Antonio, says the accident was unavoidable. The brigantine was almost under his bows when she was first seen. She sank about 10 miles off the Delaware lightship. Her crew remained on the City of San Antonio until yesterday, when they were landed here. The lost vessel was bound from Manzanilla, Cuba, for this port with a cargo of sugar and molasses. She measured 233 tons, and was built in 1873 at Calais, Maine, where her owners, the Boardman Brothers, reside.

Copyright 1879/1880/1881/1883/1884/1887/1889/1895/1913/1918 by The New York Times Company. Reprinted by permission.

NAME: <u>ADELINE</u>

DATE SUNK: December 9, 1824

REPORTED POSITION WHERE SUNK: Cape Henlopen

MASTER AT TIME OF SINKING: Captain Israel

NAME:	ADELINE TOWNSEND
RIG:	Schooner
REGISTERED NUMBER:	751
DATE & LOCATION BUILT:	1854; Pough Keepsie, New York
DATE SUNK:	January 12, 1909 Collision with Steamer Mohegan
REPORTED POSITION WHERE SUNK:	Cape Henlopen
OWNER:	Captain James H. Hogan of Jersey City; Henry Habens, Agent, 116 Broad Street
MASTER AT TIME OF SINKING:	6 persons aboard including Captain H. Thornflem of Brooklyn; all 6 were lost
CARGO AT TIME OF SINKING:	lumber
HOME PORT:	New York, New York
LAST PORT SAILED FROM:	Westport, Virginia
PORT BOUND FOR:	New York, New York
CONSTRUCTION:	231 tons gross; 219 tons net length 113.0'; breadth 30.9'; depth 9.6'
OTHER DATA:	

"Annual Report of the U.S. Life Saving Service" the following is stated:

"Wreckage from this vessel, which had been sunk in collision with the Steamer Mohegan, January 12, 1909, washed ashore, and the keeper notified the revenue cutter Mohawk, which went out and secured the spars of the lost vessel. These were hauled out on the beach by the surfman. The crew of 6 men of the ADELINE TOWNSEND were lost in the collision. A yawl, evidently from the wreck of the ADELINE TOWNSEND, was discovered on the beach by the patrol. This boat, together with hatches, oars, and a trunk of clothing was washed ashore near the station and was taken in charge by the keeper."

Also see the New York Times article of January 16, 1909. The ship was also nicknamed the "Ghost of New York".

NAME: AFRICAN QUEEN

RIG: Tanker

REGISTERED NUMBER: ON0576; Registered in Liberia, Signal: ELSM

DATE & LOCATION BUILT: 1955; Kielor Howaldtswerke A.G. in Kiel, Germany

DATE SUNK: December 29, 1958

REPORTED POSITION WHERE SUNK: Ran aground and broke in two; bow section is ten miles off of Ocean City; stern section salvaged.

Old "C" Loran 52613   38°09'04"
                   27024   74°57'15"

OWNER: African Enterprizes, Ltd; Packet Shipping Corporation, 39 Broadway, New York 6, New York

MASTER AT TIME OF SINKING: Captain Kia Danielson and 47 crew members; all rescued by helicopters

CARGO AT TIME OF SINKING: 156,000 gallons of Crude Oil

HOME PORT: Monrovia, Liberia

LAST PORT SAILED FROM: Cartagena, Columbia

PORT BOUND FOR: Paulsboro, New Jersey

WEATHER CONDITIONS AT TIME OF SINKING: gale, rain, wind from northwest

PHOTOGRAPH &/OR DRAWING: Mariners Museum photo PB20352

CONSTRUCTION: steel; 560.8' length; beam 74.1'; draft loaded 32'; registered draft 41'; powered by steam turbines; superstructure aft. 13,800 tons

OTHER DATA: Charter boat "Taurus" Captain Ed Brex; and "Good Time Diver" Captain John Steffey out of Ocean City know exact location. 210' of the bow section lies upside down in 75' of water and extends up a slope to 55'; about 30' of water over the wreck at shallow point; visability usually about 15 to 20'; abundance of fish; interior of compartments fairly intack.

The following is the Captain's statement made to the The Baltimore Sun: Wednesday Morning, December 31, 1958, page 24

Clearly exhausted, peering through bloodshot eyes, Captain Danielsen said he was awake most of last night, but was asleep shortly before 6 a.m. He said he was awakened by rough seas and ordered the speed of his tanker reduced to 4 knots.

He declined to answer a question as to whether he was off course, saying only that "The ship broke in two. That's what caused the trouble."

The 590 foot tanker separated forward of amidships, he said, with the bow "whipping around" at an angle of 45 degrees. The separated sections began bumping together very heavily, he said, "ripping one tank after another". Oil was pouring into the sea.

The crew put out fenders to keep the separated portions of the vessel from striking sparks the captain said, but he noticed smoke arising each time they slammed together.

He ordered all smoking stopped. Boilers were shut off and lights were put out.

The crew was ordered aft, he said, because that section of the vessel was most likely to remain afloat.

Captain Danielsen described it as fortunate that the break was ahead of amidships. If it had been further astern, he speculated, there would have been casualties.

First efforts to reach the Coast Guard by radio were made at about 6:10 a.m., he said, but was unsuccessful. Then distress calls were sent through a portable transmitter.

The Coast Guard said it received the first call at 7:58 a.m.

"Excellent Work"
Captain Danielsen expressed gratitude for the "excellent work" of the Coast Guard and the other services.

His own men, he said, reacted very well. There was no panic.

Subdued when they first arrived here, the crewmen of the AFRICAN QUEEN showed little emotion at their narrow escape.

In fact, James Law, 31, a Welshman now living in Germany, said he was awakened by "the impact" and started to go back to sleep.

"Then the watchman says to me 'What are you doing in bed? We're aground'" Law said. He said he could hear the aft portion of the vessel "banging" on the sandbar.

Xaver Kock, 33, the third engineer of the stricken tanker, had an interest in the vessel deeper than that of most crewmen. He said he helped build her at Kiel in 1955.

Recalling his reaction after the vessel began to break up, Paul Kunath, 35, an engine repairman, said he remembers most vividly the "cat screaming like a little kid."

He was in the engine room, he recalled, when the ship "shuddered like crazy." Lights went out and the vessel tilted.

Siegfried Barz, 20, who said he is assigned as a helmsman, reported he was on his way to "call the messman" to begin breakfast when the tanker "ran aground."

The captain ordered "full astern," he reported, and he tried to hold the vessel steady while an attempt was made to "back off".

Most of the crew reached shore bearing only small handbags that contained cameras, shaving gear and a few articles of clothing.

They also brought along "Suzy," a kitten of questionable parentage, and a small, white furry pup variously called "Bos'n" or "Napoli" by different masters. The latter name, one seaman said finally, came from the fact that the pup was acquired at a bar in Naples.

As soon as Federal officers had cleared the crew early tonight, several members promptly collapsed on the cots provided by the local civil-defense agency in the gymnasium of Ocean City Elementary School, Baltimore Avenue and Third Street.

Reprinted from The Baltimore Sun 1958-1984, The Baltimore Sun Company

Courtesy of the Mariners Museum, Newport News, Virginia 23606

NAME: AGNES MANNING

RIG: Schooner (Centerboard)

REGISTERED NUMBER: 106400; Signal Letters: KDGS

DATE & LOCATION BUILT: March, 1886; Bath, Maine by New England Shipbuilding Company

DATE SUNK: November 20, 1889

REPORTED POSITION WHERE SUNK: Near Fenwick Island

OWNER: Amos Birdsall, New Jersey

MASTER AT TIME OF SINKING: C. Birdsall (1 person lost)

CARGO AT TIME OF SINKING: coal

HOME PORT: Perth Amboy, New Jersey

LAST PORT SAILED FROM: Baltimore, Maryland

PORT BOUND FOR: New York, New York

WEATHER CONDITIONS AT TIME OF SINKING: clear

CONSTRUCTION: 876 gross tons; 4 masts, 832.86 net tons; length 185.6'; beam 38'; depth 17.4'; framing = 30" o.c.; oak, hackmatach, yellow pine; galvanized iron fastenings

OTHER DATA: New York Times, November 23, 1889 claims she "went on to Philadelphia"; but U.S. Life Saving Service records claim she was sunk, as well as Bath Marine Museum, Mariners Museum, Newport News, Virginia

AGNES MANNING

Courtesy of the Maine Maritime Museum,
243 Washington Street, Bath, Maine 04530

NAME: ALFRED

RIG: Brig or Hemaphrodite brig

REGISTERED NUMBER: 61; Signal Letters HBCP

DATE AND LOCATION BUILT: March, 1861, Baltimore, Maryland

DATE SUNK: January 21, 1882

REPORTED POSITION WHERE SUNK: off the coast of Delaware

OWNER: A.B. Morton and Sons

MASTER AT TIME OF SINKING: 8 persons lost

CARGO AT TIME OF SINKING: sugar

HOME PORT: Baltimore, Maryland

LAST PORT SAILED FROM: Demarara, South America

PORT BOUND FOR: New York, New York

CONSTRUCTION: 295 tons; length 115.1';
                             breadth 26'; depth 10.4'
                             Materials - oak; yellow pine;
                             iron and copper fastenings;
                             sheathed with yellow metal;
                             draft 12'

OTHER DATA: This vessel had a history of
                             frequent repairs; classed 1-1/2
                             for 3 or 4 years at a time.

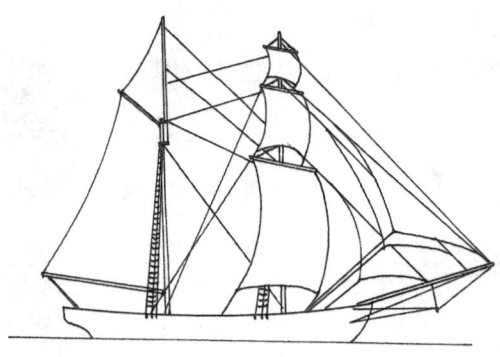

Hermaphrodite brig

NAME:	ALLIE H. BELDEN
RIG:	Schooner
DATE SUNK:	March, 1888
REPORTED POSITION WHERE SUNK:	Ashore near Cape Henlopen
REFERENCES & SUPPORTING DATA:	Lewes Lifesaving Station reported this ship and also appears in "Strange Tales From Nova Scotia to Cape Hatteras".

NAME:	ANNA AND ELLA BENTON
RIG:	Schooner
REGISTERED NUMBER:	105120; Signal Letters JLMP
DATE & LOCATION BUILT:	1872, Tuckahoe, New Jersey
DATE SUNK:	September 10, 1889
REPORTED POSITION WHERE SUNK:	1/2 mile northeast of North Beach Station in Ocean City, Maryland (beached)
MASTER AT TIME OF SINKING:	Captain Edwin C. Sharp and 4 persons; all 5 saved by wading ashore as schooner was high on beach
CARGO AT TIME OF SINKING:	none
HOME PORT:	Sommers Point, New Jersey
LAST PORT SAILED FROM:	New York, New York
PORT BOUND FOR:	Norfolk, Virginia
WEATHER CONDITIONS AT TIME OF SINKING:	heavy northerly gale
CONSTRUCTION:	137 gross tons; 130.51 net tons length 93.9'; breadth 28.3'; depth 7.9'

NAME: ANNA MURRAY

RIG: Schooner

REGISTERED NUMBER: 107466; Signal Letters KPFD

DATE & LOCATION BUILT: 1899; Camden, Maine by H. M. Bean

DATE SUNK: February 17, 1902

REPORTED POSITION WHERE SUNK: 38°35'30"N, 75°03'24"W
                                     also listed as one mile south of
                                     Indian River Inlet about 200 yards
                                     off beach and again reported as
                                     2-1/2 miles south of Life Saving
                                     Station - placing her about
                                     1-1/2 miles above inlet

OWNER: Timothy J. Mory

MASTER AT TIME OF SINKING: Captain Queen

HOME PORT: New York City, New York

LAST PORT SAILED FROM: Boston, Massachusetts

PORT BOUND FOR: Baltimore, Maryland

CONSTRUCTION: 1,534 gross tons; 4 masts;
                                     1,334 net tons; length 225';
                                     breadth 43'; depth 21.6'; double
                                     decks; oak; yellow pine; iron and
                                     copper fastenings

NAME: ANNIE E. GALLUP

RIG: Steamer

REGISTERED NUMBER: American

DATE SUNK: February 21, 1918

REPORTED POSITION WHERE SUNK: Delaware Capes

CONSTRUCTION: wood, 131 gross tons, 74 net; fishing service; 116.6'

OTHER DATA: carried in MVUS list until 1919

NAME: ANNIE T. RULAND

RIG: Small Sloop

REGISTERED NUMBER: 105868

DATE AND LOCATION BUILT: 1874; Brooklyn, New York

DATE SUNK: foundered; October 20, 1904

REPORTED POSITION WHERE SUNK: off Fenwick Island

CARGO AT TIME OF SINKING: fishing trip

HOME PORT: New York, New York

CONSTRUCTION: 7 tons; length 31.0'; width 12.0'; depth 3.8'

OTHER DATA: two persons on board; one lost

NAME: ARIEL

RIG: Brig

DATE SUNK: August 20, 1785

REPORTED POSITION WHERE SUNK: Assateague Beach

CONSTRUCTION: 200 tons

NAME: ATLANTIC

RIG: Schooner

DATE SUNK: August 9, 1843

REPORTED POSITION WHERE SUNK: on the outside tip of Cape Henlopen

MASTER AT TIME OF SINKING: Captain M'Farland

CARGO AT TIME OF SINKING: cargo saved

LAST PORT SAILED FROM: Philadelphia, Pennsylvania

PORT BOUND FOR: Barbados

CONSTRUCTION: wood

OTHER DATA: reported as gone to pieces
                                       shortly after grounding ashore

NAME: AUSTERLITZ

REGISTERED NUMBER: German

DATE SUNK: January 12, 1828

REPORTED POSITION WHERE SUNK: off Assateague

NAME: BALTIMORE

RIG: Ship

DATE SUNK: November 29, 1753

REPORTED POSITION WHERE SUNK: Great Gull Shoals
                                       Assateague Beach

OWNER: Stewart & Bowley of Baltimore

MASTER AT TIME OF SINKING: Captain Alex Stewart (lost)

CARGO AT TIME OF SINKING: pewter and linens

WEATHER CONDITIONS
AT TIME OF SINKING: northeast gale, 20' seas

CONSTRUCTION: 180 tons

NAME:	<u>BARNEGAT</u>
RIG:	Barge
REGISTERED NUMBER:	167578
DATE SUNK:	March 31, 1942
REPORTED POSITION WHERE SUNK:	37°33'30"N 75°24'15"W (in 75' of water; possibly in Virginia waters)
OWNER:	Southern Transportation Company, Commercial Trust Building, Philadelphia, Pennsylvania (Delaware Corp.)
HOME PORT:	Philadelphia, Pennsylvania
PHOTOGRAPH &/OR DRAWING:	Mariners Museum Photo PJ.232, Virginia State Archives
CONSTRUCTION:	wood; length 214.4'; breadth 32.0'; depth 14.3'; (from tonnage deck to bottom of hold); enclosure on top deck capacity is 1,288 tons; plain bow; round stern; single deck; no mast
OTHER DATA:	sunk by enemy action

BARNEGAT
Courtesy Virginia State Library and Archives

NAME:	BAYLIES WOOD
RIG:	Schooner
REGISTERED NUMBER:	3208; Signal Letters JWHM
DATE AND LOCATION BUILT:	August 1882, East Boston by R. Crosbie & Son
DATE SUNK:	April 3, 1887
REPORTED POSITION WHERE SUNK:	Cape Henlopen
OWNER:	Samuel H. Walker
MASTER AT TIME OF SINKING:	Coombs
HOME PORT:	Tawnton, Massachusetts
CONSTRUCTION:	3 masted centerboard tern with single deck and beams; 592 tons; length 150.4'; breadth 35.5'; depth 15.4'; materials: various hardwoods, hackmatack, oak, yellow pine, iron and copper fastenings

NAME:	BEAULIEU
REGISTERED NUMBER:	(French)
DATE SUNK:	August 30, 1802
REPORTED POSITION WHERE SUNK:	ashore on Assateague Beach

NAME: BERTHA

RIG: German Ship

DATE SUNK: December 31, 1886

REPORTED POSITION WHERE SUNK: stranded ashore 6 miles south
                                of Indian River Inlet on Fenwick
                                Island

CARGO AT TIME OF SINKING: railroad iron, 5,000 empty
                                petroleum barrels, 1,000 casks
                                of cement

LAST PORT SAILED FROM: Hamburg, Germany

PORT BOUND FOR: Philadelphia, Pennsylvania

CONSTRUCTION: 1,269 tons

OTHER DATA: one person lost; eighteen persons
                                aboard

New York Times
January 7, 1887

ASHORE ON AN ISLAND
Story of the wreck of the German Ship Bertha

Philadelphia, Jan. 6 - The office of Theodore Ruger and Company was filled with a large number of German sailors this morning. They were Carl Legat, second mate, and 17 men from the German ship Bertha, bound from Hamburg to this port, which stranded at Fenwick's Island, off the coast of Maryland, last Friday. The second mate said that they sailed from Hamburg on November 20 and had fine weather until December 30, when it shut down thick and rainy, and on the following morning the lookout reported land ahead. The weather was at that time intensely thick and the wind was blowing fresh from the northeast. The lead was over the starboard bow, and it was found that the water was shoaling up rapidly. Orders were given to let go the anchor, which was done immediately, but it would not hold the unfortunate ship, and she drove up on the island with a terrific crash, which shook her from stem to stern. The masts made a lurch forward, but sprang back to their places again like whalebone. All the vessel's lifeboats but one were washed away, and for hours the crew clung to the rigging with the surf constantly breaking over them and freezing to their clothing.

Finally it was agreed to launch the last lifeboat and attempt to pull for the shore. This was done, and all the crew but Lars Johannsen, who was lost while attempting to get into the boat, reached the shore after an hour's pull. The Bertha and her cargo, which consists of 5,000 empty petroleum barrels, 800 tons of scrap iron, and 1,000 casks of cement, will probably prove a total loss. The vessel is fully insured in Germany. All the crew except four have been shipped home on the German ship Hudson. The others will be kept to certify as to the way the ship was lost. The Captain and first mate remained by the vessel.

Copyright 1879/1880/1881/1883/1884/1887/1889/1895/1913/1918 by The New York Times Company. Reprinted by permission.

NAME:	BETSEY RICHARDS
RIG:	Schooner
DATE SUNK:	September 13, 1843; also reported as September 11, 1843 (ran aground)
REPORTED POSITION WHERE SUNK:	north slope of the Delaware Breakwater
MASTER AT TIME OF SINKING:	Captain Bradley of Milford, Delaware (lost) crew saved
LAST PORT SAILED FROM:	Fall River, Massachusetts
PORT BOUND FOR:	Philadelphia, Pennsylvania
OTHER DATA:	went to pieces shortly after running aground

NAME:	**B. F. MACOMBER**
RIG:	Oil Screw (Medhaden Steamer, later converted to diesel)
REGISTERED NUMBER:	211175
DATE AND LOCATION BUILT:	March 18, 1913; Robert Palmer & Son Shipbuilding & Marine Railway Company of Noank, Connecticut
DATE SUNK:	foundered on July 20, 1946 (Lloyd's lists it as a "collision")
REPORTED POSITION WHERE SUNK:	1.1 miles; 100° true north from Harbor Refuge Light, Cape Henlopen, Delaware in 60' of water
EXACT POSITION:	38°48'46"N verified by Loran 75°04'25"W
OWNER:	Consolidated Fisheries Company, Lewes, Delaware
MASTER AT TIME OF SINKING:	30 man crew
HOME PORT:	Wilmington, Delaware
PHOTOGRAPH &/OR DRAWING:	Mariners Museum Photo No. PB-20813
CONSTRUCTION:	257 gross tons; 107 net tons; length 138.1'; breadth 22.4'; depth 11.8'; 690 horsepower engine; built for fishing service
OTHER DATA:	she was taken in tow but sank 1 mile east of Harbor of Refuge Light

B.F. MACOMBER

Courtesy of the Mariners Museum, Newport News, Virginia 23606

NAME:	H. M. S. BOSTON
DATE AND LOCATION BUILT:	1692, Boston, Massachusetts
DATE SUNK:	March 1, 1695
REPORTED POSITION WHERE SUNK:	42 miles off Maryland coast, Lat. 38°10'
CONSTRUCTION:	32 guns

NAME:	H. M. S. BRAVE
DATE SUNK:	April 12, 1806
REPORTED POSITION WHERE SUNK:	30 miles off Assategue
CONSTRUCTION:	74 guns, 1,890 tons
OTHER DATA:	captured from French 2/6/1806 foundered

NAME:	S. S. BRINKBURN
RIG:	Steamer, Screw Schooner
DATE AND LOCATION BUILT:	1880; Newcastle, England by C.S. Swan & Company
DATE SUNK:	between 1887 and 1888; listed as "stranded"
OWNER:	R. Bell
DRAWING:	
CONSTRUCTION:	1,938 tons; <u>iron</u>; 280'0" long; 34'8" beam; 24'5" depth; 200 horsepower C.J. 2 cylinder engine, 32" and 62" x 42"; 2 decks (one iron) plus one open tier of beams 5 bulkheads; water ballast; double bottom aft; engine built by R&W Hawthorn, Newcastle

NAME:	BUENA VISTA
RIG:	Brig
DATE SUNK:	October 31, 1853
REPORTED POSITION WHERE SUNK:	ashore on the inside tip of Cape Henlopen
LAST PORT SAILED FROM:	Philadelphia, Pennsylvania
PORT BOUND FOR:	Wilmington, North Carolina

NAME:	CADET
RIG:	Schooner
REGISTERED NUMBER:	September 23, 1839 in New York City
DATE AND LOCATION BUILT:	1833 in Dennis Creek, New Jersey
DATE SUNK:	February 9, 1842
REPORTED POSITION WHERE SUNK:	on beach near Delaware Breakwater
OWNER:	unknown
MASTER AT TIME OF SINKING:	Captain Claypool (crew went ashore in lifeboat and carried to lighthouse)
HOME PORT:	Bridgeton, New Jersey
LAST PORT SAILED FROM:	Virginia
PORT BOUND FOR:	New York
WEATHER CONDITIONS AT TIME OF SINKING:	heavy northwest winds
CONSTRUCTION:	71 tons

NAME: CALINARCHER

RIG: Yacht

DATE AND LOCATION BUILT: unknown

DATE SUNK: December 3, 1942

REPORTED POSITION WHERE SUNK: Delaware Breakwater

OWNER: Charles Crowninshield, New
                                     York City

MASTER AT TIME OF SINKING: Charles Crowinshield, William
                                     Rogers, Roy S. George, New York
                                     City, Brooklyn, New York

CARGO AT TIME OF SINKING: none

HOME PORT: New York

LAST PORT SAILED FROM: New York

PORT BOUND FOR: Miami, Florida

WEATHER CONDITIONS
AT TIME OF SINKING: craft was anchored and drifted
                                     up against breakwater

CONSTRUCTION: 45' long; 2 masts

DATA: New York Times
                                     December 14, 1942

NAME: CANCEAUX

DATE SUNK: 1772

REPORTED POSITION WHERE SUNK: burned offshore Assateague Beach

NAME: CANTON BRITON

DATE SUNK: January 1, 1867

REPORTED POSITION WHERE SUNK: Delaware Breakwater

HOME PORT: New York

LAST PORT SAILED FROM: New York

PORT BOUND FOR: Havana, Cuba

NAME: CARPENDER
                                   (formerly Schooner-Barge
                                   No. Twenty-Five)

RIG: Steel Schooner-Barge

REGISTERED NUMBER: 203545

DATE AND LOCATION BUILT: 1906, Camden, New Jersey

DATE SUNK: foundered December 12, 1933

REPORTED POSITION WHERE SUNK: 38°22'12"N near Ocean City,
                                   Maryland - 9 miles; 74°58'55"W
                                   offshore

OWNER: P.F. Martin Barge Corporation
                                   of Delaware, 111 Walnut Street,
                                   Philadephia, Pennsylvania

CARGO AT TIME OF SINKING: coal

HOME PORT: Phildadelphia, Pennsylvania

LAST PORT SAILED FROM: Hampton Roads, Virginia

PORT BOUND FOR: South Amboy, New Jersey

CONSTRUCTION: 1,566 gross tons; 1,520 net
                                   tons; length 227.0'; breadth
                                   38.1'; depth 19.6'

NAME:	CARRIE A. BUCKMAN
RIG:	Schooner
REGISTERED NUMBER:	126089; Call Letters KBCF
DATE AND LOCATION BUILT:	1882; Verona, Maine
DATE SUNK:	April 6, 1889
REPORTED POSITION WHERE SUNK:	at the point of Cape Henlopen
MASTER AT TIME OF SINKING:	Captain Stubbs and 7 crew; all 8 persons saved
CARGO AT TIME OF SINKING:	sugar and logwood
HOME PORT:	Bucksport, Maine
LAST PORT SAILED FROM:	San Domingo, W. I.
PORT BOUND FOR:	New York, New York
CONSTRUCTION:	273 tons net; 287.19 tons gross; length 128.0'; breadth 29.2'; depth 10.5'

NAME:	CARRIGAN
RIG:	Schooner
REGISTERED NUMBER:	13389; Call Letters H.L.P.C.
DATE AND LOCATION BUILT:	1862; Chester, Pennsylvania
DATE SUNK:	March 29, 1903
REPORTED POSITION WHERE SUNK:	at point of Cape Henlopen
MASTER AT TIME OF SINKING:	Captain Primrose and 7 persons; all 8 saved
CARGO AT TIME OF SINKING:	lumber
HOME PORT:	Philadelphia, Pennsylvania
LAST PORT SAILED FROM:	James River, Virginia
PORT BOUND FOR:	New York City
CONSTRUCTION:	221 tons gross; 176 tons net; length 109.2'; breadth 29.0'; depth 9.2'

NAME: CASPIAN

RIG: Oil Screw (trawler)

REGISTERED NUMBER: 202929; WA 3448

DATE AND LOCATION BUILT: 1906; Essex, Massachusetts

DATE SUNK: March 16, 1953

REPORTED POSITION WHERE SUNK: 48 miles east of Assateague
                                       Island or 52 miles southeast of
                                       Ocean City, Maryland

OWNER: Aspen Fish and Products Company
                                       New Jersey
                                       Richardson Channel & Rio Grande Road
                                       Wildwood, New Jersey

MASTER AT TIME OF SINKING: 7 man crew

HOME PORT: Philadelphia, Pennsylvania

CONSTRUCTION: 94 gross tons; 78 net tons
                                       length 88.5'; width 22.6';
                                       depth 10.4'; 100 horsepower engine

DATA: Lloyd's weekly casualty report
                                       states that the fishing vessel
                                       "Maris Stella" rescued 7 man crew
                                       from Trawler "CASPIAN". Coast
                                       Guard conducted search for vessel
                                       52 miles southeast of Ocean City,
                                       Maryland. The crew was
                                       transferred to U.S.C.G.C.
                                       "Gentian" which proceeded to
                                       Cape May.

NAME: CASEY and BROWN

RIG: Oil Screw (clam dredge)

REGISTERED NUMBER: 267339

DATE AND LOCATION BUILT: 1954; Tampa, Florida

DATE SUNK: November, 1975 (Coast Guard report received 5/8/75; investigation still pending - 1978)

REPORTED POSITION WHERE SUNK: 2-1/2 miles northeast of Indian River Inlet

OWNER: Sea Harvest Inc., New Jersey
                                   1044 New York Avenue, Cape May, New Jersey 08204

HOME PORT: Philadelphia, Pennsylvania

CONSTRUCTION: steel; length 64.8'; breadth 20.0'; depth 7.5'; 79 gross tons; 205 horsepower engine

DATA: lays intack and upright at about a 45° angle in 40' of water on a sand and gravel bottom; visability usually poor 3' to 6'; heavy mussel growth covers plating.

NAME: CASTEL

RIG: Brig

DATE AND LOCATION BUILT: unknown

DATE SUNK: June 23 or 28, 1841

REPORTED POSITION WHERE SUNK: just south of Ocean City, Maryland on the beach

MASTER AT TIME OF SINKING: crew saved

LAST PORT SAILED FROM: Bristol, Maine

PORT BOUND FOR: Turks Island

NAME:	C. B. HAZELTINE
RIG:	Ship (built as a ship; converted to a bark in 1882; back to ship in 1884)
REGISTERED NUMBER:	5302; Signal Letters HJMW
DATE AND LOCATION BUILT:	November 1859 by C. P. Carter, Belfast, Maine
DATE SUNK:	March 12, 1888
REPORTED POSITION WHERE SUNK:	foundered near Hen and Chicken Shoal
OWNER:	Welcome Gilkey
MASTER AT TIME OF SINKING:	4 lost (owner was master)
CARGO AT TIME OF SINKING:	coal
HOME PORT:	New York City, New York
LAST PORT SAILD FROM:	Philadelphia, Pennsylvania
PORT BOUND FOR:	Boston, Massachusetts
CONSTRUCTION:	wood; 880.5 gross tons; 836.54 net tons; length 155.5'; breadth 33.8'; depth 22.3'; draft 19'; double decks; oak, yellow pine, iron and copper fastenings; yellow metal sheathing

NAME:	CELESTE
RIG:	Schooner
REGISTERED NUMBER:	126881
DATE AND LOCATION BUILT:	1892; Prince George County, Virginia
DATE SUNK:	January 10, 1903
REPORTED POSITION WHERE SUNK:	1-3/4 miles N.N.E. of Green Run Inlet Station
MASTER AT TIME OF SINKING:	Captain Payne and 6 persons; all 7 saved
CARGO AT TIME OF SINKING:	guano
HOME PORT:	Tampa, Florida (Norfolk, Virginia in 1901)
LAST PORT SAILED FROM:	New York City, New York
PORT BOUND FOR:	Baltimore, Maryland
CONSTRUCTION:	41 tons gross; 24 tons net; length 74.3'; breadth 18.6'; depth 5.7'

NAME:	**U.S.S. C. F. SARGENT**
RIG:	Schooner - barge
REGISTERED NUMBER:	125283; Call Letters JPRH
DATE & LOCATION BUILT:	1874; Yarmouth, Maine
DATE SUNK:	July 31, 1918
REPORTED POSTION WHERE SUNK:	38°41'38"N 75°00'48"W in 52' of water (Hen and Chicken Shoal)
OWNER:	Edward Luckenbach
HOME PORT:	New York
PHOTOGRAPH &/OR DRAWING:	Mariners Museum photo - PK 3681
CONSTRUCTION:	1,689 tons; length 220'; breadth 41.3'; depth 17.9'
DATA:	Sprung leak and grounded on shoal.

NAME:	CHAMPION
RIG:	Steam Packet (sidewheeler)
REGISTERED NUMBER:	4899
DATE AND LOCATION BUILT:	1859; Wilmington, Delaware by Harlan and Hollingsworth
DATE SUNK:	November 8, 1879
REPORTED POSITION WHERE SUNK:	Cape Henlopen (15 miles from Delaware Lightship)
OWNER:	New York and Charleston S.S. Co. from 1867 to 1879
MASTER AT TIME OF SINKING:	31 lives lost (16 passengers and 39 crew onboard) Captain R. W. Lockwood (saved)
CARGO AT TIME OF SINKING:	general
HOME PORT:	New York City, New York
LAST PORT SAILED FROM:	New York City, New York
PORT BOUND FOR:	Charleston, South Carolina
WEATHER CONDITIONS AT TIME OF SINKING:	calm, bright night
PHOTOGRAPH &/OR DRAWING:	Mariners Museum photocopy of Harper's Weekly sketch
CONSTRUCTION:	iron; 1452 tons; length 235'; depth 18'; double vertical beam engine, cylinders are 42" x 10' stroke; two boilers; accommodations for 388 cabin passengers and 350 steerage passengers; machinery built by Harlan & Hollingsworth
OTHER DATA:	Collided with the British bark "Lady Octavia"; struck on starboard side near cat head

New York Times
Monday, November 10, 1879

The Loss Of The Champion
Stories told by those who were saved.
Six survivors on the Bark Petit Codiac

The terrible scene on the sinking steamship - Three men hanging to a sky-light - Mr. Garner's buoyant hat.

The bark Petit Codiac, from the Delaware Breakwater, for New York, reached this port yesterday afternoon, bringing six survivors of the wreck of the Charleston steam-ship Champion that was sunk in a collision with the English ship Lady Octavia, off the Delaware Capes, early on Friday morning. Three of these survivors were cabin passengers; one, a colored man, was a steerage passenger, and two belonged to the Champion's crew. The four passengers were the only passengers saved out of the sixteen on board. They gave the same account of the disaster, in general, as was given in yesterday's Times: That the Champion left this port for Charleston last Thursday afternoon, with 16 passengers and a crew of 39; that the weather was clear and the sea smooth; that, after midnight, the moon and stars were shining; that, at 3 o'clock in the morning, while the moon was still shining brightly, the steam-ship came in collision with the Lady Octavia, the latter striking her on the starboard side near the cathead, and that the steam-ship sank in 14 fathoms of water, in less than 5 minutes after the collision. The Octavia left the Delaware Breakwater on Thursday morning bound for this port. At the time of the collision she was making northward under a full sail as the Champion was steaming southward at the rate of about 10-1/2 knots an hour. The vessels met so nearly bow on that a very slight variation of course on either hand would have broken the force of the shock. The Octavia remained near the spot for several hours after the collision and her boats picked 27 of the Champion's officers and crew out of the water. The steam-ship sank so quickly after the meeting that many of those on board of her had not time even to buckle on life preservers. The cause of the collision is still unknown, the Captain of each vessel laying the blame upon the shoulders of the other and probably nothing but an official investigation can determine the responsibility. The three cabin passengers who were saved were all kept afloat by a sky-light from the wreck, and were picked up, nearly exhausted, by one of the Octavia's boats. The colored steerage passenger, who was saved, sprang overboard and reached one of the rescuing boats. The scene just as the steamship went down is described by the rescued passengers as terrible almost beyond belief. Only two names can be taken from the list of the lost - that of William Slake, who had bought a ticket, but had afterward sold it to G.E. Garner, one of the three rescued cabin passengers, and that of Luke Kelly, a fireman, whose name was duplicated yesterday. Mr. Siska is safe on shore, and the death list is reduced to 30. Appearances indicate that the crew took active measures for their own safety. 50 per cent of the steamer's men having been saved, while only a trifle over 25 percent of the passengers were rescued. Five of the passengers were women, and they were all lost. Following is a list of the passengers and members of the crew who were lost, and those who were saved:

List of the saved:
Passengers Charles E. Garner, New York, cabin passenger; Joseph Mitchell, New York, cabin passenger; Martin Broad, New York, cabin passenger; J. B. Heran, New York, steerage passenger; J. B. Foster, New York, steerage passenger; five crew; C. E. Bause, first assistant engineer; Catherine Cross, stewardess; Charles Ehler, seaman; William Farrell, fireman; Patrick Flynn, fireman; John Foster, porter; Isaac Hammond, chief cook; George Holland, waiter; Frank Jacobson, seaman; Edward Jones, fireman; Luke Kelly, fireman; R. W. Lockwood, Captain; Frederick Mackman, seaman; Charles Miller, second mate; Richard Owen, cabin boy; Moses Pinckney, waiter; Wesley Reeve, Chief Engineer; Alexander Rose, coal passer; Frederick Richard, seaman; John M. Thompson, seaman - 20

List of the lost:
Passengers - cabin - Stuffany, W. W. Clark, William Peets, Mrs. O. D. Andrews, Charleston; Miss Mikel, Charleston, H. Huxbable, Boston; Mrs. H. Huxbable, Boston; steerage - C. Patton, P. Patton, Kate Machney, Rose Barber - 11; Crew - John B. Moffet, purser, R. H. Leonard, first mate; C. F. Siltes, carpenter, Paul Hahn, seaman; John Nelson , seaman; James F. Anderson, seaman; John Allan, boy; Casper Poberg, 2nd assistant engineer; A. F. Potts, oiler; Frank Pettit, seaman; Mike Savage, fireman; August Winters, stoker; Frank Carrigan, stoker; William Curten, stoker; Peter Sewalls, steward; Andrew Middleton; John Richardson, 2nd cook; Daniel Gjarden, pastry cook; Antonio Wishard, pastry cook. The total number of board was 55, of whom 10 were cabin passengers, 6 steerage passengers and 39 crew. Of the cabin passengers, 3 were saved; of the steerage passengers 2, and of the crew 20; 7 cabin passengers were lost; 4 steerage passengers and 19 of the crew. The room D2 in the "Social Hall" which was described yesterday as sold, but not called for, was engaged by Mr. J. L. Marvin, but he reached the pier about 5 minutes after the steamship had sailed and is now safe on shore.

Mitchell's Struggle in the Water

Joseph Mitchell, of this City, one of the survivors, reached this city yesterday afternoon on the bark Petit Codiac. He is a young sporting man who was on his way to Columbia, S.C. to get "tips" on the races. Several things happened, he says, at the time of starting, which caused him to fear that the trip would be attended by misfortune. He had bought a ticket for the ship Gulf Stream, but had to change to the Champion. The gang-plank slipped down and got fastened in the paddles of the wheel, and this delayed the boat two hours. The ship-carpenter, who lived in Orange, N.J. came to the ship Thursday morning, just to take a look at it, having told his family that he would be home that night. The company suddenly decided to send the Champion instead of the Gulf Stream, and impressed him for the trip. "He didn't get home that night" said Mitchell, "and will never get home." When Mitchell went to bed that night he was nervous and couldn't sleep, and he kept his clothes on. At 3 a.m. he looked out of a port-hole near the head of his bed and saw that the night was bright and clear. He then went to sleep. He was awakened by a crash, and the noise of persons running past his room and screaming for help. He jumped up and ran out. When he got into the corridor, the ship was sinking, and standing at an angle of 45 degrees, stern up, bow down. He ran up the incline, and soon found himself at the helm on the hurricane deck. "A number of persons were clinging," said he, "to the life-boats begging the sailors for God's sake to cut them loose." The sailors had all they could do to look out for themselves. No one appeared to be in command. I heard no orders, and saw no attempts to help others. It was each one for himself. Those who were clinging to the life-boats went down with them when the ship sank. The vessel was sinking so fast, and was standing so straight, that I had to hold on to the stern railing to keep myself from slipping down into the water. At last down she went. So powerful was the sudden jar that it shook loose all of our holds and down we went along the slippery deck into the water. The sunction drew us all down, and when we came up we had to grab for anything floating in reach. I don't know how long I was down, but when I got to the surface some one had a terrible grip on my arm. We went down again together. I managed somehow to get loose and again arose to the surface. I had but little sense left, not enough to save myself. But a big wave lifted me and threw me high and dry. When I fell I lit upon a window sash. I fell flat upon it, and my knees, arms, and hands went through the glass, cutting me all up; but I clung to the sash, and being a good swimmer, when I fully recovered my senses, was able to float. Along came a man floating on a chair. He wanted my sash, because it was flat and his chair kept rolling. I had to fight him off, and I cut myself many times more on the glass. Then another man, floating on a tub, came along. He wanted my sash. Then I had to defend it against two. It was bright and clear, and I could see the boats floating around picking up persons. The man on the chair, the man on the tub, and myself yelled for help. There were barrels, boxes and furniture bobbing around us, and we were in danger of having our brains knocked out every minute. It was awful cold, and I was fast getting benumbed, and my throat was full of salt water. One of the life-boats passed us for the second time without coming to our help, and then I despaired and gave up, and became unconscious. The next thing I knew, a big sailor was lifting me up over the side of the Lady Octavia, and was soon afterward pouring hot coffee down my throat. The Lady Octavia was badly stove herself, and when the bark Petit Codiac came in sight, the signal of distress was given, and she came up to us. The bark brought four passengers, E.G. Garner, Martin Broad, J.B. Foster, and myself, and two sailors, John Thompson and Charles Ebler, to New York. We reached Court Street, Brooklyn, between 2 and 3 o'clock this afternoon. C. Staffany was lost. The girl, Miss Mary Mikel, who was returning from Europe with her mother, Mrs. O.A. Andrews, of Charleston, S.C. was very beautiful, and about 17 years of age. Even when we poor fellows were fighting for life in the waves, more than one man asked what had become of her, and everyone of us looked around for a trace of her, and had any one of us seen her he would have saved her or died trying to do it. I guess she never got out of her cabin. I don't see how the collision could have occurred without carelessness on the part of the Champion's officers. The night was so bright and clear that we could recognize friends in the waves, and see small boats a long way off. I think no one could have been on watch, because if anyone had been he couldn't have helped seeing the Lady Octavia."

Mr. Garner's Story

Mr. Charles E. Garner, of No. 19 East Twelfth Street, was one of the rescued passengers brought to this port in the bark Petit Codiac. He was starting on a Southern canvassing tour for his firm, C.E. Garner & Co., advertising agents of No. 5 Clarke Street. He was going first to Charleston, and thence through a large part of the South, intending to spend the entire Winter there, and he was accompanied by a colored valet, J.B. Foster, who was booked in the steerage. Mr. Garner's name was not on the passenger list, hence he was not reported among the lost, saved, or missing yesterday. William Siska, whose name was given yesterday in the saloon list, had bought a first class ticket for Charleston, entitling him to Berth 2 in Room No. 22; but before the steamer sailed he changed his mind and his ticket was sold, through a third person, to Mr. Garner. The latter gentleman, however, did not give notice of the change to the purser, and it was supposed that Mr. Siska was occupying the place for which he had paid. Mr. Garner left a widowed mother at home, two sisters, and a brother, who knew that his ticket was issued in Mr. Siska's name. When, therefore Siska was put among the drowned in yesterday morning's reports, they gave up Mr. Garner for lost; but the house of mourning was changed into one of gladness when, yesterday afternoon, the son and brother walked into the house, safe and sound. Mr. Garner was found by a TIMES reporter last evening just as he came out of the water, except that he was not wet. He is a very pleasant and intelligent young gentleman, and he had as narrow as escape as possible "My valet, Foster", said he, "belonged in the steerage, but he did not like the appearance of things there and would not sleep there but lay down on deck alongside the smoke-stack. I had a bottle of brandy along, and had made the acquaintance of several of the passengers, among them Mr. Broad, and we had been playing cards the evening before. My room opened off the saloon, and I was in bed and asleep when the accident happened. I felt a slight concussion, which partly awakened me, but it was not very much of a shock. I think I might have gone to sleep again if I had not heard the confusion on deck. I got up and put on my pantaloons and vest; and tried to open my cabin door, but the key had dropped out, and it took some time to find it. When I got the door open, I saw ladies dressing hurriedly in the saloon, so I went on dressing myself. I put on my vest and my coat and overcoat both together, having taken them off together, and would have put on my shoes and stockings, but I could not find them. My boy came down to my room and I asked him whether we could save the samples, for I had two large sachels full of samples, and we did not think there was any immediate danger, or at least we thought that they would get the boats out. Foster said he thought we could save them, so he took one and I took the other, and we went on deck and were soon separated. I would like to describe the scene on deck, but I could never do it. It was a horrible one, and I saw in a minute that the only chance was to get hold of something that would float and jump overboard before the ship went down. A large part of the forward deck was under water. She was sinking bow first, and her bow was already so far down in the water that her deck slanted very much. The stern being up in the air. Everything movable was sliding and rolling down, and those on board were shrieking and crying for help, and trying to climb up the hilly deck. Some of them clawed at the planks in their terror, but they only slid downward

toward the water. It did not take long to see that the boats could not
be launched, for there were no axes at hand, and there was no time to
lower them. There was no time to spare, for the bow was settling lower
in the water every minute. In coming through the saloon I had seized a
light chair, the handiest buoyant thing I happened to see. I had kept
this in my hand; so, seeing that the ship was about to sink, I dropped
the sachel from my other hand, held the chair in front of my breast, and
sprang overboard. I hoped by going overboard at that time to get far
enough away to avoid the suction caused by the ship when she went down,
but I was too late. I was hardly in the water, with my frail and almost
useless life-preserver, when the steamship went down. I heard a few
cries and then there was a great rushing of water that seemed like a
deep river running straight down to the bottom of the sea, and I was
engulfed with all the rest, and went down I can't say how far enough, at
any rate, almost to take the breath out of me, and when I came to the
surface again I was very nearly gone. But I had a life-preserver with
me on that trip that helped me to the surface quicker, I think, than I
would otherwise have come. Here it is." Mr. Garner took from the top
of the piano a black derby hat of the present style. "You see," he
continued, "the lining has not been wet. I put it on when I came out of
my stateroom and just as I was about to jump overboard I gave it a
tremendous pull almost down over my eyes. It was on so tight that it
did not come off when I went down, and the crown-being, of course, full
of air - was as good as a small life-preserver, and helped me to the
surface. When I came up into the air again the ship was gone. There
were things floating about, but out of my reach. Near me were three
men, floating, holding up their hands and crying to someone to save
them. One of them, who was nearest me, seized me by the shoulder, but I
was nearly dead myself, and did not expect ever to see land again, and I
took his hand off my shoulder and clung to my chair. Within the next
two or three minutes I saw all three of these men go down and never come
up again. They were all drowned. I floated around a short time on my
chair, with the aid of some swimming, and after a while I saw two men
holding to something that seemed to support them. It was bright
moonlight and starlight and not at all foggy, as has been said, and I
saw that one of the men was Mr. Broad. I swam over to where they were,
still keeping hold of my chair, and found that they were clinging to a
piece of skylight about six feet long and two feet wide with most of the
glasses broken. I took hold of the skylight too, but it was almost as
frail a support as my chair. Mr. Broad recognized me and he said: "I
wish we had some of that brandy here now, Garner." "I said I wished we
had too, but the wishing didn't do any good. By this time the Octavia
was a long way off. We seemed to be drifting very fast in some current
that was carrying us away from the ship. There was no boat in sight,
and it was hard work holding onto the skylight. It cut our hands, and
we were all very nearly exhausted. We floated in this way a long time,
and several times I was so far gone that I had serious thoughts of
letting go and letting myself drown. At last we saw a small boat. It
seemed to be about a mile and a quarter away. We shouted as loud as we
could, and thought they heard us, for they came toward us but before
they reached us they turned about. They did this several times, and
almost discouraged us. I said that we must all shout together, to make
as much noise as possible, and we did. That time they heard us, and the
boat came up to us. It was just in time, for Mr. Mitchell, the third
man on the sash, was very badly frightened, and kept trying to climb up

on the sash, although we told him several times that if he persisted he would surely drown us all for the sash was useful only when we kept as much of our bodies under water as possible. "Mr. Broad was pulled into the boat first" Mr. Garner continued, "and he was no sooner in than he shouted to me. "Here's your darky, Garner." I held up my arm and was drawn in next, and sure enough, there was Foster. I never expected to see him again when we were parted on the deck. The boat had picked up some of the crew, and we were soon taken aboard the Octavia. They did everything they could for us there. Captain Johnson of the Octavia is deserving of great credit, for he was not sure that his own ship was not sinking; but he stayed at the scene of the disaster for several hours, picking up everybody he could find. If he had not done so, I think we would all have been lost. Ben Foster, my boy, tried his best to save my sachel of samples. He jumped overboard with it, and he declares that it carried him right straight to the bottom, for it was way heavy. When he struck bottom, he says, he left go the sachel, and he soon came up. Some of the currents took him in a different direction from that in which I went, and he was picked up by the Octavia's boat. Aboard the Octavia they gave us some stray articles of clothing, for some of us were rather scantily clothed. The water was not rough, but not entirely smooth, and it was not very warm." Mr. Garner says there were life-preservers in his state room, but he thought they would take to the boats, and so did not put one on. Some of the crew, he says threw a pile of life-preservers on the deck, but these were all gone before he left the saloon. He thinks that considerably more than five minutes must have elapsed after the collision before the steamer went down. Mr. Garner's hands were cut in a number of places by holding on to the floating sky-light. He says that he will take a new start for Charleston, but that he will try it this time by rail.

What the Chief Engineer Says

Wesley Reeve, chief engineer, who is now at his home, No. 152 Oakland-Avenue, Brooklyn, tells the following story: "I had just got asleep, when I was aroused by a great noise and crash. I at once jumped out of bed, threw open my door, and looked out. My room was situated midway between the upper and lower engine rooms, and in full view of both. Charles F. Bunce, first assistant engineer, was at the engines. I saw him at his post, and put on my pantaloons and shoes and went down to the lower engine room. Bunce ordered the oiler to see if any water was coming into the ship. The oiler replied "Yes, very bad." Bunce then ordered the large donkey pump at work, and it was started by the oiler and Casper Foberg, second assistant engineer. I then went back and put on my coat and hat. In the meantime the signal to back the engines was given, and the ship was being backed. In two minutes from the time I was first aroused, the water drove us out. It was our duty to stay at the engines as long as we could, and we did stay. When the signal is given to stop the engines, as it was given at the time of this crash, the first thing the firemen do is to throw open the furnace doors. There were six furnaces down there. The water rushed in so fast that it flowed up into the red-hot furnaces and came up in dense and fatal volumes of steam. The steam drove us off. We were on the main deck. When we had to leave, the ship was going down bow first, and was standing at an angle of 45 degrees. We all rushed aft on the main deck and when we reached the quarter deck ascended to the hurricane or top deck. When I reached the hurricane deck, all was confusion. The vessel was settling so fast that there was already water there. I grabbed a lounge and I had no sooner got hold of it than the water floated it and me off. The ship went down almost straight, and all the loose freight came shooting up along the main deck with fearful velocity. When I was floating, the stewardess, Catherine Cross, of Charleston, S.C. stood upon the deck and she cried out "What shall I do?" some one shouted to her "Jump for your life, Kate." She jumped into the sea, caught hold of a box and floated until she was picked up. Three lady saloon passengers were drowned. They never got even to the surface. The Captain aroused them and told them for God's sake not to wait to dress. But they did wait and were drowned. Catherine Cross says she saw one of them leave her room dressed in a night-gown and a shawl, and then, after walking a few steps in the corridor, return to her room for more clothes. That was the last of her. The boats were all loose, but could not be handled owing to the inclination of the ship. The life-raft was loose, and it floated off all right with many persons clinging to it. On the hurricane deck was a spare small boat, which floated off bottom side up. It had a pair of oars fastened in it. This boat floated past me, and I mounted it. It was pretty dark and among the many dark objects that were just visable in the water you couldn't tell a man's head from one of the thousands of cabbages that were floating around. But you could hear men and women crying for help on all sides, and all were clinging to life-preservers or floating parcels. While on the upturned boat, I saw something floating. I soon found it was a human being, and made for it. It was Bunce. I pulled him out. The life-raft was near and it came toward us. At this time the second mate and the chief cook were the only occupants of it. They soon afterward found the Captain floating around and picked him up. He had gone down with the ship, remaining by the main rigging giving orders until the last moment. When the life-raft came alongside the boat, Bunce got off and I righted her. We then got in her and put off. We picked up Frederick Mackman, Luke Kelly and William Farrell, who were floating around with nothing on but their shirts. We put them on a life-raft, and went out a second time and picked up George Holland, John Thompson, and Alexander Rose. The water was so cold that Rose was already insensible. After putting them on the raft, we went out again. We heard some poor fellow cry out loudly for help. His voice came from afar. We looked for him for over an hour, but could find no trace of him. In the meantime, the Octavia's boats had been working bravely. When we gave up finding any more persons, we all went aboard the Octavia, except four passengers and two sailors, who went aboard an unknown passing bark on its way to New York. We were struck just forward of the foremast. There was not much of a jar, but the Octavia just cut into us. The crew slept forward, and just behind them was the steerage. The Octavia must have cut right into the steerage, for although many of the crew were saved, not a steerage passenger has since been seen, except one colored man who had happened to stay up all night. The Octavia was badly cut, but the cutting was all just in front of a water tight compartment, and it did not endanger her. I can't say who was at fault, for R. H. Leonard, who was on watch, was lost, and cannot give evidence. Many of the saved were hurt by the floating packages. The Captain was badly hurt in the back; Kelly had his forehead and cheek laid open, and I received a few bruises. But we're glad to get off with our lives."

Copyright 1879/1880/1881/1883/1884/1887/1889/1895/1913/1918 by The New York Times Company. Reprinted by permission.

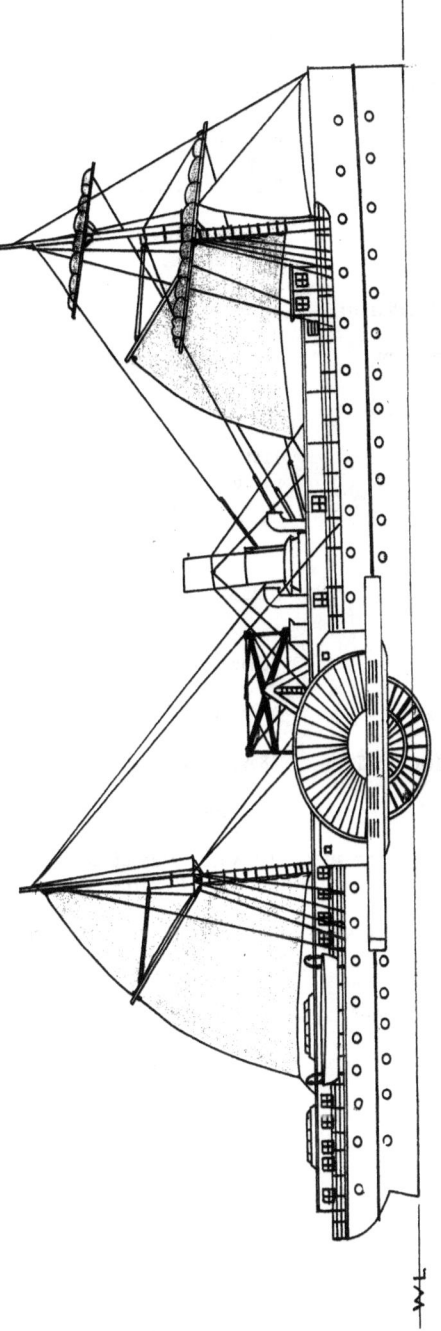

CHAMPION
outboard profile

NAME:	CHARLES P. SINNICKSON
RIG:	Schooner
REGISTERED NUMBER:	125109
DATE AND LOCATION BUILT:	unknown
DATE SUNK:	September 17, 1876
REPORTED POSITION WHERE SUNK:	6 miles south of Cape Henlopen
CARGO AT TIME OF SINKING:	railroad ties
LAST PORT SAILED FROM:	Richmond, Virginia
PORT BOUND FOR:	Philadelphia, Pennsylvania
OTHER DATA:	listed as partial loss; four persons lost

NAME:	CHARLES P. STICKNEY
RIG:	Schooner
REGISTERED NUMBER:	4975; Call Letters HDVF
DATE AND LOCATION BUILT:	1859; Philadelphia, Pennsylvania
DATE SUNK:	September 10, 1889
REPORTED POSITION WHERE SUNK:	350 yards west of Lewes Station, 75 yards from beach
MASTER AT TIME OF SINKING:	Captain Kendall and 5 persons (all 6 saved by breeches bouy)
CARGO AT TIME OF SINKING:	coal
HOME PORT:	Philadelphia, Pennsylvania
LAST PORT SAILED FROM:	Philadelphia, Pennsylvania
PORT BOUND FOR:	Norfolk, Virginia
CONSTRUCTION:	188 tons; 2 masts; 178.87 tons net length 108.6'; breadth 27.8'; depth 9.0'
OTHER DATA:	she parted her chains and drove ashore completely breaking up

NAME: CHARLOTTE

RIG: Brig
REGISTERED NUMBER: unknown
DATE AND LOCATION BUILT: unknown
DATE SUNK: November 15, 1853
REPORTED POSITION WHERE SUNK: ashore at Delaware Breakwater
CARGO AT TIME OF SINKING: coal
LAST PORT SAILED FROM: Philadelphia, Pennsylvania
PORT BOUND FOR: Boston, Massachusetts

NAME: CHATTAHOOCHEE

RIG: Brig
DATE AND LOCATION BUILT: 1840; Kingston, Massachusetts
DATE SUNK: December 18, 1846
REPORTED POSITION WHERE SUNK: Lewes, Delaware (struck at foot of causeway)
MASTER AT TIME OF SINKING: Captain Freeman
CARGO AT TIME OF SINKING: coal
HOME PORT: Registered in New York City; October 13, 1844
LAST PORT SAILED FROM: Philadelphia, Pennsylvania
PORT BOUND FOR: Boston, Massachusetts
CONSTRUCTION: 115 tons

NAME:	U.S.S. CHEROKEE 458 (formerly the EDGER F. LUCKENBACK)
RIG:	U.S. Navy Tug
REGISTERED NUMBER:	458
DATE AND LOCATION BUILT:	1891 by John H. Dialogue & Sons, Camden, New Jersey (commissioned into the Navy 12/5/17)
DATE SUNK:	February 26, 1918 (foundered)
REPORTED POSITION WHERE SUNK:	12-1/2 miles off Fenwick Island; Light Vessel Tanker "British Admiral" picked up survivors (12), 2 died before reaching port
EXACT POSITION:	Latitude 38°36'14"N, Longitude 74°39'37"W (converted from Loran C)
OWNER:	United States Navy
MASTER AT TIME OF SINKING:	Lieutenant E. D. Newell of Philadelphia 28 lives lost, (5 officers, 23 crew)
CARGO AT TIME OF SINKING:	none
HOME PORT:	Philadelphia Navy Yard
LAST PORT SAILED FROM:	Newport, Rhode Island on February 24, 1918
PORT BOUND FOR:	Washington, D.C.
WEATHER CONDITIONS AT TIME OF SINKING:	full gale from northwest
PHOTOGRAPHY &/OR DRAWING:	Mariners Museum Photo of a Sketch No. PBI13872 and Peabody Museum of Salem, Massachusetts
CONSTRUCTION:	272 tons; length 120'; breadth 24'6"; draft 15'
OTHER DATA:	July, 1977, Wreck is intack in 95' of water and is upright; all portholes have been removed; the bottom is sand and visability is usually about 30'; charter boat captains out of Ocean City, Maryland and Indian River Inlet, Delaware know exact location

Philadelphia Public Ledger
Saturday Morning, April 20, 1918

INQUIRY IS ORDERED ON CHEROKEE LOSS
Navy Board Finds Grounds to Warrant Investigation by Higher Tribunal

(Public Ledger Bureau, Washington, April 19)

The board of investigation which inquired into the causes for the loss of the naval tug CHEROKEE February 26, causing the deaths of Lieutenant E. D. Newell, of Philadelphia, and twenty-six men, has reported that it found sufficient grounds for an investigation by a board of inquiry, it was stated officially today by the Navy Department.

The board of investigation heard witnesses in connection with the allegations of the widow and other relatives of Lieutenant Newell that he knew the vessel to be unseaworthy, had so reported to his superiors and had objected to making the fatal trip which resulted in the tug being lost off the Maryland coast.

Under judicial procedure in the Navy, a court of inquiry sits only when the lower body finds sufficient grounds in its investigation for further action. The court of inquiry is expected to begin hearings at Philadelphia within a day or two. There is one higher tribunal in the naval establishment, a court-martial, which would try officers found by the lower bodies to have been negligent in the discharge of duty.

The investigation into the CHEROKEE's loss was ordered by Secretary of the Navy Daniels, following the publication by the Public Ledger of Mrs. Newell's charges that her husband had insisted the vessel was unseaworthy.

The New York Times
February 28, 1918

29 LOST AT SEA AS NAVAL TUG SINKS

The CHEROKEE, Formerly Luckenback Craft, Lost Off Maryland Coast
Ten Survivors Landed
British Steamers Bring Into Philadelphia Men Picked Up From Rafts

Philadelphia, PA - Twenty-nine are believed to have lost their lives yesterday morning when the seagoing naval tug CHEROKEE foundered in a gale off the Maryland coast.

Ten survivors and the bodies of eight other members of the crew of thirty-nine were brought here today on two British ships and landed at the Navy yard. No trace of the remaining members of the crew was found. Among those missing is Junior Lieutenant Edward D. Newell, commander of the tug. Ordinarilly, the CHEROKEE carried forty but one man was not aboard. According to the Captain of one of the rescue ships, the primary cause of the disaster was the breaking of the steering gear. A fifty mile northeast gale was blowing at the time and the little vessel was at the mercy of high seas. Two rafts were launched and the crew abandoned the ship as she was about to founder.

"I saw wreckage about six miles from the scene of the disaster," said the Captain. "Later I found an upturned boat and then we sighted the raft on which there were twelve men. We took them all aboard and two died from exposure."

"I saw six bodies and summoned another vessel to pick them up as I wanted to give assistance to the living men."

Virtually all the twelve men on the raft were unconscious when picked up. There were four men on the second raft. Two were washed overboard and the other was dead.

The wireless man aboard the CHEROKEE stuck to his post to the end. The wireless operator at the Naval Research Station at Cape May, New Jersey picked up the first call from the tug yesterday morning. Later the signals became indistinct and soon ceased.

The CHEROKEE was formerly the tug Edgar F. Luckenback and is said to have been bound from an Atlantic port to Norfolk for repairs.

U.S.S. CHEROKEE

Courtesy of Peabody Museum, East India Square, Salem, Massachusetts

NAME: CITY OF GEORGETOWN

RIG: Schooner

REGISTERED NUMBER: 127709

DATE AND LOCATION BUILT: November 1902 at Bath, Maine
                                   by William Rogers
                                   (this is the last vessel he built)

DATE SUNK: February 2, 1913 at 12:32 a.m.

REPORTED POSITION WHERE SUNK: 38°47'04"N,
                                   74°33'50"W in 90' of water

OWNER: Pardon G. Thompson in 1913

MASTER AT TIME OF SINKING: A. J. Slocum (1906-1913)
                                   all 8 persons on board saved)

CARGO AT TIME OF SINKING: salt

HOME PORT: New Bedford, Massachusetts

LAST PORT SAILED FROM: New York

PORT BOUND FOR: Savanah, Georgia

WEATHER CONDITIONS
AT TIME OF SINKING: good breeze

PHOTOGRAPH &/OR DRAWING: Mariners Museum Photo RK1115

CONSTRUCTION: 599 gross tons; 506 net tons;
                                   length 168.7'; beam 36.4';
                                   depth 12.6'; white oak, yellow
                                   pine; 4 masts (see details
                                   of construction survey)

OTHER DATA: Collision with German S.S. Prinz
                                   Oskar; crew of Georgetown launched
                                   a dory and were picked up by
                                   Prinz Oskar.

New York Times
February 2, 1913

Liner and Schooner Crash and Wooden Craft Sinks
Crew of Eight Are Saved

Passengers of the Prinz Oskar Shaken From Their Bunks by Impact Rush Onto Decks

Philadelphia, Feb. 2 - Hidden from each other by the powerful glare of a lightship until they were too close to turn aside, the Hamburg-American liner, Prinz Oskar and the four-masted schooner, City of Georgetown, met in collision forty miles at sea early this morning. The schooner sank in a few minutes, and her Captain and crew of seven were saved only by the display of the greatest gallantry. The Prinz Oskar came back to port today with a heavy list, made by water which had poured in through a big hole in her port bow.

The collision took place off the Five Fathom Bank Lightship, due East of the Delaware Capes. The Prinz Oskar, emerging from the Delaware Breakwater, was making a wide circle past the lightship to reach the regular transatlantic lane,. The schooner, carrying full sail in a good breeze, was coming down the coast with a cargo of salt from New York for Savannah and was keeping close to the lightship in order to get her bearings.

The ships came together at 12:55 a.m., three minutes before they had sighted each other. As the liner veered from the lightship, the watch upon the bridge beheld the schooner. The log of the Prinz Oskar sets the time at 12:52. With the cry from the watch, the signal bells sounded in the engine room of the Prinz Oskar and the propellers were reversed at full speed astern.

The helmsman of the schooner, seeing the liner, shouted orders to the watch to cut sails loose and threw the wheel about. A gust of wind caught the sails, and spread them out; however, before the crew could sever the ropes, the schooner, with her bowsprit stretching in front like a battering ram, struck the Prinz Oskar. Through the steel plates the bowsprit jammed its way, carrying the Prinz Oskar's huge port anchor ten feet into the forecastle. Sailors asleep in their berths were jerked to the floor amid shattered fittings and ice. The impact was so powerful that the steel liner was rocked. Passengers were thrown from their bunks. At the same time, the four masts of the schooner snapped off and fell to the deck with the mass of spars, sails and rigging. For a few minutes, the wooden ship and the liner were locked fast by the bowsprit. Then the engines of the liner pulled her free, jerking the bowsprit from its fastenings. As the steamer backed, the schooner settled at the bow. With the decks in a tangle and the vessel rapidly sinking, Captain A. J. Slocum and his crew of seven men had a hard time to save themselves. They were able, however, to launch a dory and get away just as the craft sank. The boat was almost swamped by the suction of the sinking vessel, and four of the men who had tried to cling to it while the others rowed were drawn into the whirlpool. They clung to wreckage, however, and were picked up by lifeboats from the liner after hope of saving them had almost been abandoned.

Captain Von Teuenfeig, who was on the bridge at the time of the accident, took prompt measures to reassure the three first class cabin and thirty steerage passengers aboard. Stewards shouted that the Prinz Oskar was in no danger. Despite the assurances, many of the passengers fled to the decks scantily clad, braving the blasts of icy wind. They were soon calmed.

The Prinz Oskar dropped anchor off Gloucester at 1:45 o'clock. Her passengers and cargo will be discharged tomorrow morning, and the steamship will be docked for repairs. The City of Georgetown was built in Bath, Maine, in 1902 and hailed from New Bedford. She was 170 feet long, 40 feet beam, and had a capacity of 1900 tons.

Copyright 1879/1880/1881/1883/1884/1887/1889/1895/1913/1918 by The New York Times Company. Reprinted by permission.

CITY OF GEORGETOWN

Courtesy of the Mariners Museum, Newport News, Virginia 23606

NAME:	CITY OF ORLEANS (named for Gulf States cities)
RIG:	Auxiliary schooner barge, formerly 5 masted barkentine; Auxiliary engine removed in 1922 and cut down to Schooner-barge in 1923.
REGISTERED NUMBER:	217696 documented May 6, 1919; Hull No. 10
DATE & LOCATION BUILT:	Launched February 13, 1919 at International Shipbuilding Company, Orange, Texas
REPORTED POSITION WHERE SUNK:	Offshore Fenwick Island; 5 miles SW x W 1/2W; 241° 52'30"T of Fenwick Islands Lightship in 6 to 7 fathoms; in tow of tug "Underwriter"; later reported as 13 miles SE x S off Fenwick Islands Coast Guard Station; 38° 21'27"N 74° 53'50"W
DATE SUNK:	November 14, 1923 Vessel abandoned by crew at 6:00 a.m. November 13; last seen afloat at 5 p.m. November 14
OWNER:	Transferred to Italian registry in June, 1919 while at Gulfport; transferred to William F. Probst, Staten Island, New York (Smith and Terry, Inc. agent) in June, 1922.
MASTER AT TIME OF SINKING:	H.C. Riggs - 3406 Lafayette Blvd, Norfolk, Virginia and 4 crewmen (no loss of life)
CARGO AT TIME OF SINKING:	coal - 5,187 tons
HOME PORT:	New York, New York
LAST PORT OF CALL:	Hampton Roads, Virginia
PORT BOUND FOR:	Boston, Massachusetts
WEATHER CONDITIONS AT TIME OF SINKING:	Heavy N.E. gale; 72 m.p.h. wind; rain; heavy seas

CONSTRUCTION: Wood; 2,347 gross tons; 2,232 tons net; length 283'; breadth 45.9'; depth 22.4'; 2 - 4 cylinder oil engines (removed); single deck; poop deck = 64'; forecastle = 33'; keel 20" x 24"; Keelson 20" x 22"; deck beams 15" or 16" square; planking 4-1/2" to 8" thick, planked inboard and outboard of frames; designed by Henry Piaggio; Italian Vice-Consul at Gulfport, Miss. (City of Beaumont series)

OTHER DATA: foundered in gale, the logbook of the U.S.C.G.C. MANNING states:

On Jan 24, 1924, the U.S.C.G.C. MANNING destroyed the wreck of the CITY OF ORLEANS using 28 mines and clearing the wreck to a minimum depth over wreck of 7 fathoms. The MANNING anchored nearby at Lat. 38°20'24" N and Long. 74°54'02" W in 8 fathoms at 7:45 a.m. and finished with destruction at 3:50 p.m., using a motor whaleboat to place charges on wreck.

CITY OF ORLEANS
Courtesy Bloodsworth Shipyard

CITY OF ORLEANS

spare anchor lashed to deck

wooden bench affair triatic stay from foremast is attached

large wood ballard

vertical capstan

raised deck over forecastle

boat davits

Plan View of Forecastle

steering gear is a massive worm gear assembly

Side View

Top View

INTERNATIONAL SHIPBUILDING CORP

1-1/2" raised letters

iron steering wheel

Not to Scale

triatic stay

wooden bench affair on forecastle

Side View

Front View

CITY OF ORLEANS
Skematics of deck details

NAME: CLEOPATRA

RIG: Steam Screw

REGISTERED NUMBER: 4255

DATE & LOCATION BUILT: 1865 at Fairhaven, Connecticut by Samuel P. Hook

REPORTED POSITION WHERE SUNK: 8 miles off Delaware Lightship

DATE SUNK: October 29, 1889 (last seen afloat with decks awash 1 hour after collision)

OWNER: International Steamship Company (1884 to 1889) Charter to Old Dominion S.S. Co.

MASTER AT TIME OF SINKING: Captain Dale and 24 crewmen (no one lost)

CARGO AT TIME OF SINKING: 900 bales of cotton

HOME PORT: Boston, Massachusetts

LAST PORT OF CALL: West Point, Virginia

PORT BOUND FOR: Philadelphia, Pennsylvania

WEATHER CONDITIONS AT TIME OF SINKING: Clear - good weather

PHOTOGRAPH &/OR DRAWING: Mariners Museum Photo P.B. 28099

CONSTRUCTION: 1,045 tons; length 184'; beam 40'; depth of hold = 23'; also listed as 191' x 43'x 18'; wood construction; vertical direct acting engine, cylinder 46" x 3' stroke; single screw

OTHER DATA: She collided bow onto bow with the "Crystal Wave" and again hit the stern of the "Crystal Wave" 20 feet from stern. She was uninsured.

New York Times
Thursday, October 31, 1889

TWO STEAMERS SUNK
AN EXTRA ORDINARY COLLISION OFF THE DELAWARE LIGHTSHIP

A collision occurred on Tuesday morning about eight miles off the Delaware Lightship between the Old Dominion steamship Cleopatra and the excursion steamer Crystal Wave. Both vessels were lost, but the crews were rescued by the Old Dominion steamship Kanawha, which landed them at this port yesterday.

The Crystal Wave had recently been purchased by Capt. K. S. Randall of Washington, and was on her way to that city under command of Capt. Samuel Martin, a well-known coast pilot of good standing. The Cleopatra was bound from West Point, Va. for this city, with a cargo of 900 bales of cotton, and under the command of Capt. Dale. It was fine weather off the Capes of Delaware early on Tuesday morning, and daylight had begun to steal in among the light clouds in the eastern sky when the lookout upon the Cleopatra discovered on the port bow the red lights of an approaching steamer, which proved to be the Crystal Wave. The Cleopatra kept on her course, and a few moments later her officers were surprised to see the red light disappear and a green light appear in its place.

The Crystal Wave seemed to be coming directly toward the Cleopatra, and as a collision seemed imminent, the latter vessel went to starboard in the hope of avoiding the danger. But this movement proved of no avail. An instant later, the two vessels crashed together. They struck bow to bow and then rebounded. Then they came together again, the Cleopatra crashing into the Crystal Wave about twenty feet from her stern and cutting into her hull. The Cleopatra in the meantime had received fatal blows below her water mark. After the second crash the two vessels drifted slowly apart. It was discovered that the Cleopatra was filling rapidly, and Capt. Dale ordered the boats to be lowered. Several boats were hurriedly launched from the Cleopatra and one was sent to the Crystal Wave to see if help was needed by that vessel, which was sinking rapidly. Her crew, however, were launching their boats. Two of these were smashed while being got into the water, but her entire crew of thirteen men succeeded in getting into the boats which were successfully launched.

A few moments after they had rowed away from the Crystal Wave that vessel careened and sank out of sight. She went down about fifteen minutes after the collision occurred. In the meantime the Cleopatra was filling rapidly. Her upper decks only remained above water, these having been kept up by the cargo of cotton. Her crew of twenty-six men were all in their boats, which lay within hailing distance of those of the Crystal Wave.

The rapidly increasing daylight showed to the distressed sailors an approaching steamer which had evidently discovered them. This proved to be the Kanawha, bound from Newport News for this port. An hour after the collision the Kanawha came up and the crews of the lost vessels, together with several of their boats, were taken on board. Of the Cleopatra, only the hurricane deck aft and the main deck forward were now above water. An attempt was made to take her in tow but it was found that the latter was too low down in the water to be towed by the Kanawha and the attempt was abandoned. The Kanawha then proceeded on her voyage. It is possible that the Cleopatra is still buoyed up by her cotton, and is floating with her upper decks just at the water's edge. In this case, she will be apt to prove a dangerous obstacle to passing vessels.

The Crystal Wave was built in Greenpoint in 1875 and registered 588 tons. For a number of years she ran on the Bridgeport line and was known as a very fast steamer. During the past two seasons she has run on one of the Rockaway excursion lines. She started from this port last Saturday, but owing to threatening weather returned to the Highlands, where she remained until Monday, when she resumed her voyage. It is reported that her insurance, if any, was very light.

Copyright 1879/1880/1881/1883/1884/1887/1889/1895/1913/1918
by The New York Times Company. Reprinted by permission.

Courtesy of the Mariners Museum, Newport News, Virginia 23606

NAME: COMMERCE

RIG: Merchantman (English)

DATE SUNK: 1771

REPORTED POSITION WHERE SUNK: Near Cape Henlopen

MASTER AT TIME OF SINKING: Captain Addis

CARGO AT TIME OF SINKING: very little saved

LAST PORT OF CALL: England

PORT BOUND FOR: New York

NAME: CORNELIA

RIG: Merchantman

DATE SUNK: 1757

REPORTED POSITION WHERE SUNK: Cape Henlopen

MASTER AT TIME OF SINKING: Captain Smith

LAST PORT SAILED FROM: Philadelphia, Pennsylvania

PORT BOUND FOR: Gibralter

NAME: CREW LEVICK NO. 5

RIG: Barge

REGISTERED NUMBER: 167894

DATE & LOCATION BUILT: June 1920 by Tank Shipbuilding Corporation in Newburgh, New York

REPORTED POSITION WHERE SUNK: S.S.W. 14 miles Fenwick Shoal Lightship
38°12'45"N; 74°50'40"W

DATE SUNK: April 11, 1923

OWNER: Henry L. Doherty Company in 1921

MASTER AT TIME OF SINKING: crew of 2, both saved

CARGO AT TIME OF SINKING: in ballast

HOME PORT: New York

PORT BOUND FOR: Philadelphia, Pennsylvania

CONSTRUCTION: steel; length 160'; beam = 36'; depth = 10.2'; 5 watertight bulkheads; oil carrier; al barge; river and harbor service; 513 gross and net tons

OTHER DATA: foundered; insured for $60,000; in tow of tug "S.S. Halo"; from logbook of U.S.C.G.C. "KICKAPOO" April 12, 13, 1923 - "sunk oil barge CREW LEVICK NO. 5" by gunfire.
Lat. 38°12'45"N, Log. 74°50'40"W"

NAME: CRICKET

RIG: Barge

DATE SUNK: September 28, 1890

REPORTED POSITION WHERE SUNK: Five Fathom Bank, Delaware

NAME:	CRYSTAL WAVE
RIG:	Steam Sidewheel
REGISTERED NUMBER:	125420
DATE & LOCATION BUILT:	Greenpoint, 1875
DATE SUNK:	October 29, 1889
REPORTED POSITION WHERE SUNK:	8 miles from Delaware Lightship
OWNER:	formerly a Bridgeport Line Steamer then a Rockaway Excursion Steamer
MASTER AT TIME OF SINKING:	Captain Samuel Martin (pilot); 13 persons on board - no one lost
HOME PORT:	Bridgeport, Connecticut
PHOTOGRAPH &/OR DRAWING:	Mariners Museum Photo No. P.B. 516
CONSTRUCTION:	588 tons net; 777.55 tons gross; length = 203.0'; breadth = 22.0'; depth = 10'; 800 h.p.
OTHER DATA:	The CRYSTAL WAVE sank in 15 minutes as a result of a collision with the steamship CLEOPATRA. See newspaper article filed with CLEOPATRA report.

Courtesy of the Mariners Museum, Newport News, Virginia 23606

NAME: DAUPHIN

RIG: Brig
REGISTERED NUMBER: (French)
DATE SUNK: March, 1744
REPORTED POSITION WHERE SUNK: broke up on Winter Quarter Shoal
OTHER DATA: (4 saved)

NAME: DAVID H. ATWATER
                                    (Ex. CRABTREE)
                                    Later (W.J. CROSBY)
RIG: Steam Screw
REGISTERED NUMBER: 218156 (Hull 505)
DATE & LOCATION BUILT: 1919, Astabula, Ohio, June
DATE SUNK: April 2, 1942
REPORTED POSITION WHERE SUNK: 37°57'00" N Winter Quarter Shoal
                                    75°10'00" W
OWNER: Atwacoal Transportation Company,
                                    Fall River, Massachusetts
MASTER AT TIME OF SINKING: 29 man crew
PHOTOGRAPH &/OR DRAWING: Bowling Green State University
                                    Library
CONSTRUCTION: steel; 2,438 gross tons;
                                    1,468 net tons; length 253.4';
                                    breadth 43.6'; depth 25.1';
                                    1,250 h.p. engine built by Lake
                                    Erie Boiler Works, Buffalo,
                                    New York

W.J. CROSBY (DAVID H. ATWATER)

Photo courtesy of the Institute for Great Lakes Research,
Bowling Green State University

NAME:	H.M.S. DeBRAAK
RIG:	English Sloop of War
DATE & LOCATION BUILT:	1781 in Holland
DATE SUNK:	May 23, 1798
REPORTED POSITION WHERE SUNK:	Cape Henlopen in 80 feet of water
OWNER:	British Navy
MASTER AT TIME OF SINKING:	Captain James Drew and 86 officers and crew and Spanish prisoners taken from Spanish Galleon in Straits of Florida; 35 lost
CARGO AT TIME OF SINKING:	gold, coins and copper
HOME PORT:	Plymouth, England
PORT BOUND FOR:	Nova Scotia
WEATHER CONDITIONS AT TIME OF SINKING:	storm
CONSTRUCTION:	18 guns; wood
OTHER DATA:	the Sunpapers article of Wednesday, November 14, 1984 and The Maryland Beachcomber, September 21, 1984

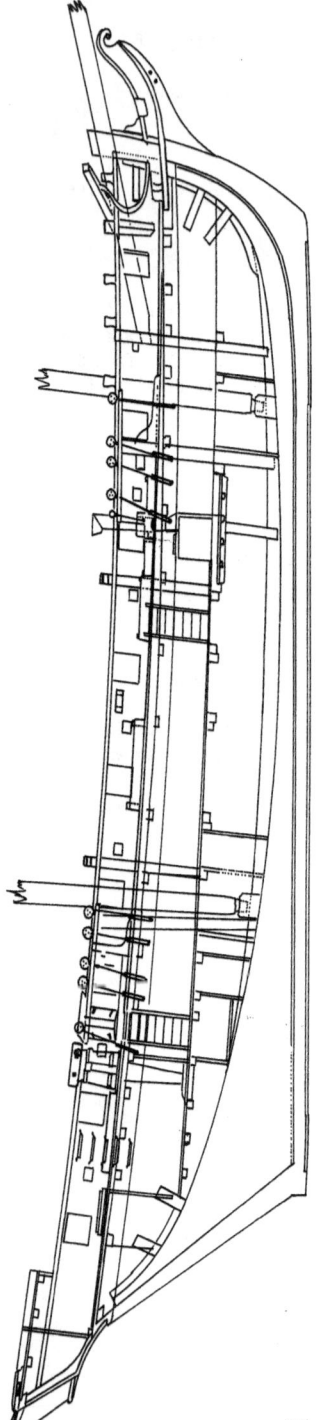

H.M.S. DeBRAAK
INBOARD PROFILE

Length on the upper deck 84'- 0"
extreme breadth 28'- 11"
depth in hold 11'- 2"

NAME:	**D. & E. KELLEY**
RIG:	Schooner
DATE & LOCATION BUILT:	1861; Bell's Ferry, New Jersey
DATE SUNK:	December 21, 1887
REPORTED POSITION WHERE SUNK:	off coast of Delaware
OWNER:	Captain Taylor
MASTER AT TIME OF SINKING:	Captain Taylor (5 persons aboard - 3 survived - Mate David H. Campbell, John W. Coleman, Frank Taylor)
CARGO AT TIME OF SINKING:	lumber
LAST PORT SAILED FROM:	Norfolk, Virginia
PORT BOUND FOR:	New Haven, Connecticut
WEATHER CONDITIONS AT TIME OF SINKING:	snow storm
CONSTRUCTION:	202 tons
OTHER DATA:	

New York Times
December 21, 1887
Page 8, Column 1

Driven Blind and Insane
Hours of Suffering for a Shipwrecked Crew
Mate Campbell's Graphic Story of the Loss of His Schooner -
The Captain and Steward Lost

Three feeble and suffering survivors out of a crew of five hearty men who sailed the schooner D. and E. Kelley out of Norfolk Harbor last Friday were brought into port yesterday by the Norwegian steamer "Oden, Capt. Define from Port dePaix. Two of the survivors were colored men - John W. Coleman and Frank. Their legs were badly swollen, and they had not yet sufficiently recovered from the effects of their trying experiences to be on their feet. The third survivor was the mate, David E. Campbell, who, although his hands were badly frostbitten, was about last evening when the Oden hauled into the Erie Basin, in South Brooklyn. Mr. Campbell, after making arrangements for the removal of Coleman and Taylor to the Marine Hospital, told the tragic story of the loss of the schooner.

The D. and E. Kelley, it seemed, had a cargo of lumber on board for New Haven. Capt. Will Taylor, an experienced skipper of Providence, was in command. On Saturday afternoon, when the vessel was 12 miles east of Phoenix Island, a heavy squall came up, and Capt. Taylor headed for the Delaware Breakwater. Soon afterward the wind shifted ahead, and in order to avoid going ashore it was necessary to put about and head out to sea. At 6 o'clock in the evening, during a terrific snow squall, the deckload shifted and the schooner was thrown on her starboard beam ends. The crew sprang into the port main chains, where they clung for life, while the vessel drifted through the blinding snow toward the shore, where she struck at 11 o'clock. A sea then washed over the port side, where the crew clung. The steward, a young colored man who had been shipped at Norfolk, relaxed his hold and was swept away. For an instant he was seen struggling, then a flurry of snow swept over him, and when the wild wind had passed away he had disappeared.

Soon afterward the deckload went overboard, carrying with it the mainmast. After being relieved of this load the schooner slowly righted, and at midnight the four survivors crawled to the quarter deck. The cabin had been swept away and the forward part of the vessel was completely under water. At 4 o'clock in the morning the wind changed to westward and the wreck floated off and drifted out to sea. When the eastern sky grew bright and the stormy waves began to assume distinct forms, the survivors began an anxious day's watch. Their supplies had been washed away, and the pangs of thirst and hunger were added to the sum of their misery. Dusk found them still watching and hoping for the succor which came not. The mate passed the gloomy watches of the stormy night in looking for the lights of some passing vessel. The two colored men forgot thirst, hunger, and exposure for the time in sleep.

Soon after midnight Capt. Taylor started up and cried out that he could not see. His suffering had resulted in blindness. Then his mind began to wonder, "I cannot see!" he cried, "I am thirsty and hungry! Have some one take me to a hotel!" Then he reached out his hands and groped for some one to lead him. The mate finally convinced him to sit down on the deck. He made a few incoherent remarks and then sank back, and his sense of suffering gave way to the peaceful calm of death. A moment later the body of the poor old Captain was washed overboard. At 3 o'clock the next afternoon the survivors were picked up by the Oden, on board of which they were treated with every kindness. Capt. Taylor was a widower. He has several children in Providence. He owned the D. and E. Kelley, which measured 202 tons and was built in 1861 at Bell's Ferry, New Jersey.

Copyright 1879/1880/1881/1883/1884/1887/1889/1895/1913/1918 by The New York Times Company. Reprinted by permission.

NAME: DEERHOUND

RIG: Schooner

DATE SUNK: March 5, 1769

REPORTED POSITION WHERE SUNK: on beach at Assateaque Island

CONSTRUCTION: 230 tons

NAME: DETERMINEE

REGISTERED NUMBER: (French)

DATE SUNK: March 26, 1803

REPORTED POSITION WHERE SUNK: Fenwick Shoals

CONSTRUCTION: 28 guns, 545 tons;
                                  length 124.5'; breadth 31.5';
                                  draft aft 14'; draft forward 12';
                                  overall length 151.5'

NAME: DORA

RIG: Schooner

REGISTERED NUMBER: 157468

DATE & LOCATION BUILT: 1896; Bath, Maine

DATE SUNK: October 1, 1915, also reported as November 13, 1915

REPORTED POSITION WHERE SUNK: Fenwick Island, Maryland southeast of Fenwick Island Lightship

MASTER AT TIME OF SINKING: 3 man crew

CARGO AT TIME OF SINKING: coal

HOME PORT: Boston, Massachusetts

LAST PORT OF CALL: Norfolk, Virginia

CONSTRUCTION: 825 gross tons; wood; 745 net tons; length 184.7'; breadth 35.1'; depth 16.5'; 3 masts

OTHER DATA: all 3 persons aboard were saved

NAME: E. BUCKMAN

RIG: Schooner

DATE SUNK: February 21, 1842

REPORTED POSITION WHERE SUNK: on the bar at Lewes, Delaware

NAME: **ELECTRIC SPARK**

RIG: Steam Screw

DATE SUNK: July 10, 1864

REPORTED POSITION WHERE SUNK: at sea off the eastern shore of Maryland; Lat. 37°33'N, Long. 74°20'W also reported as Lat. 38°26'N, Long. 73°52'W in 53 fathoms

MASTER AT TIME OF SINKING: 42 passengers (all aboard were transferred to "KELSO")

CARGO AT TIME OF SINKING: mail; miscellaneous items; money $160,000 in gold bars among ballast

HOME PORT: Philadelphia, Pennsylvania

LAST PORT SAILED FROM: New York, New York

PORT BOUND FOR: New Orleans, Louisiana

CONSTRUCTION: iron hull; 810 tons

OTHER DATA: This vessel was burned by the C.S.C. FLORIDA, Lt. Morris commanding.

NAME: ELIZA ANN HOOPER

RIG: Schooner

REGISTERED NUMBER: 8255; Call Letters JDFV

DATE & LOCATION BUILT: 1868; Smyrna, Delaware

DATE SUNK: September 10, 1889

REPORTED POSITION WHERE SUNK: 3/4 mile west of Lewes Station

MASTER AT TIME OF SINKING: Captain Sharp and 5 persons (all 6 saved)

HOME PORT: New York City

LAST PORT SAILED FROM: New York City

PORT BOUND FOR: James River, Virginia

CONSTRUCTION: 167.47 tons gross; 159.10 tons net; length 106.1'; breadth 28.1'; depth 7.0'

NAME: ELIZABETH

RIG: Ship

DATE SUNK: February 1702

REPORTED POSITION WHERE SUNK: Winter Quarter Shoals

CARGO AT TIME OF SINKING: slaves

NAME:	ELIZABETH
RIG:	Schooner
DATE SUNK:	December 18, 1846
REPORTED POSITION WHERE SUNK:	parted her chains and drove ashore above "the mole" at Lewes, Delaware
MASTER AT TIME OF SINKING:	Captain Bourne
CARGO AT TIME OF SINKING:	coal
LAST PORT SAILED FROM:	Philadelphia, Pennsylvania
PORT BOUND FOR:	Nantucket

NAME:	ELIZABETH DeHART
RIG:	Schooner
REGISTERED NUMBER:	8038; Call Letters HTRS
DATE & LOCATION BUILT:	1860; Essex, Connecticut
DATE SUNK:	July 5, 1888
REPORTED POSITION WHERE SUNK:	Point of Cape Henlopen on Round Shoal
MASTER AT TIME OF SINKING:	Captain Hunter and 5 crewmen (all 6 saved)
CARGO AT TIME OF SINKING:	laths
HOME PORT:	New York (Portland, Maine)
LAST PORT SAILED FROM:	St. John, N.B.
PORT BOUND FOR:	Washington, D.C.
CONSTRUCTION:	230 tons gross; 218.23 tons net; length 107.5'; breadth 28.6'; depth 9.9'
OTHER DATA:	Lifeboat was used from Lewes, Delaware Life Saving Station to rescue crew.

NAME:	ELIZABETH PALMER
RIG:	5 Masted Schooner
REGISTERED NUMBER:	200201
DATE & LOCATION BUILT:	September, 1903 at the Percy & Small shipyard in Bath, Maine
DATE SUNK:	January 26, 1915 after collision with steamship WASHINGTONIAN at 3:40 a.m.; still partially afloat at noon but all headgear gone according to J.S. Pruit of the Indian River Lifeboat who rode out to the wreck.
REPORTED POSITION WHERE SUNK:	1 mile southwest by south from Fenwick Island Lightship; crew was picked up by the steamship HAMILTON at 7 a.m. (14 crewmen).
EXACT POSITION WHERE SUNK:	northwest of R-2 whistle bouy; lat. 74° 49'34" north; long. 38° 27' west; (converted from Loran C coordinates 27018.5, 42414.0)
OWNER:	Palmer Fleet, Boston, Massachusetts and J.S. Winslow & Company, Portland, Maine (owner in 1911)
MASTER AT TIME OF SINKING:	Captain George A. Carlisle, Boothbay Harbor Maine
CARGO AT TIME OF SINKING:	none (in ballast) 14 persons were on board including Mrs. John Andrews, wife of the steward
HOME PORT:	Boston, Massachusetts
LAST PORT SAILED FROM:	Portland, Maine on January 10
PORT BOUND FOR:	Norfolk, Virginia
WEATHER CONDITIONS AT TIME OF SINKING:	clear, fresh north/northwest breeze; ELIZABETH PALMER heading southwest by west at 8 knots; she struck the WASHINGTONIAN on her starboard side about amidships

PHOTOGRAPH &/OR DRAWING:	Mariners Museum Photograph PR 3852
CONSTRUCTION:	wood, 3,065 tons gross; 2,446 tons net; 5 masts; length 300.4'; beam 48.3'; depth 28'3"; double beams double decks, oak frames, yellow pine and hackmatack.
OTHER:	As of 1976, bow sits upright and about 12' off sand with two anchor chains and anchors; rest of wreck is broken up and spread out and low (Coast Guard had dynamited wreck shortly after mishap.) Large timbers remain but are scattered; wreck is in three general sections. 72' to sand bottom; visibility sometimes poor; fish are plentiful but no lobsters.
DATA:	U.S. National Archives - wreck report and U.S. Livesaving Station report; Bath Marine Museum data, letter from W.J.L. Parker - author of "Great Coal Schooners of Maine", New York Times (front page, Wednesday, January 27, 1915)
NOTE:	The ELIZABETH PALMER also collided and sank the ESTELLE PHINNEY on December 27, 1907 off of Barnegat, New Jersey.

<u>Bath Daily Times</u>
January 28, 1915
(page 5, column 3)

"PALMER CAPSIZED"
Wrecked Schooner Was Being Towed Into Port

New York, Jan. 28 - A wireless message received here today from the revenue cutter MOHAWK, said that the five-masted schooner Elizabeth Palmer of Portland, Maine, capsized today off the Delaware Capes and is now breaking up. The crew had been taken off sometime before.

The PALMER, built in Bath, was in collision (sic) with the steamship WASHINGTONIAN off the Delaware Capes two days ago and became waterlogged. The
MOHAWK was towing her into the Delaware Breakwater when she capsized.

Bath Daily Times
January 30, 1915
(page 8, column 2)

"The five-masted schooner, ELIZABETH PALMER, lying on her beam ends, is pounding herself to pieces off the Fenwick Island Shoals. The revenue cutter, MOHAWK, Capt. J. L. Carden, did a good piece of work in trying to save her, but weather conditions were all against success, and it now seems as though Capt. Carden would have to blow her up to prevent her from becoming a menance to navigation."

ELIZABETH PALMER

Courtesy of the Mariners Museum, Newport News, Virginia 23606

NAME: ELLA

RIG: Schooner

REGISTERED NUMBER: 7190; Call Letters HFPG

DATE & LOCATION BUILT: 1853; Petty's Island, New Jersey

DATE SUNK: November 25, 1888

REPORTED POSITION WHERE SUNK: Rehobeth, Delaware; 1-3/4 miles north of Rehobeth Beach Coast Gulf Station (Life Saving Station) just south of Hen & Chickens Shoal, 100 yds. from shore

MASTER AT TIME OF SINKING: Captain Gates and 6 crewmen (all 7 persons saved)

CARGO AT TIME OF SINKING: lumber, laths, pickets

HOME PORT: Bangor, Maine

LAST PORT SAILED FROM: Bangor, Maine

PORT BOUND FOR: Philadelphia, Pennsylvania

WEATHER CONDITIONS
AT TIME OF SINKING: heavy northeast gale

CONSTRUCTION: wood; 193 tons gross; 183.69 tons net; length 105.6'; breadth 28.8'; depth 8.6'

NAME: EMILY A. FOOTE

RIG: Oil Screw

REGISTERED NUMBER: 135139

DATE & LOCATION BUILT: 1875; Boothbay, Maine

DATE SUNK: August 23, 1930

REPORTED POSITION WHERE SUNK: Breakwater, Harbor of Refuge

CONSTRUCTION: 113 gross tons; 75 net tons; length 109.0'; breadth 17.6'; depth 7.2'

NAME:	EMELIE E. BIRDSALL (named for the wife of Captain Jacob E. Birdsall)
RIG:	Schooner
REGISTERED NUMBER:	135010; Call Letters JPMC
DATE & LOCATION BUILT:	1874; Wilmington, Delaware by Jackson, Sharp & Company
DATE SUNK:	February 4, 1908; 2:55 a.m.
REPORTED POSITION WHERE SUNK:	off Winter Quarter Shoal 10 miles
OWNER:	Jacob H. Birdsall, Whertwon, New Jersey
MASTER AT TIME OF SINKING:	Captain Samuel Lamson, 7 persons aboard; 7 lost (also reported as 3 lost)
CARGO AT TIME OF SINKING:	railroad ties
HOME PORT:	Perth Amboy, New Jersey
LAST PORT SAILED FROM:	Norfolk, Virginia
PORT BOUND FOR:	Elizabethport, New Jersey
CONSTRUCTION:	491 wood tons (See Gov. Jackson for size particulars as both schooners were the same size); 467 tons burden; length 134.8'; breadth 33.5'; depth 12.4'; 3 masts; oak with iron fastenings
OTHER DATA:	Article in "New Jersey Courier" states that the Old Dominion steamship "JEFFERSON" collided with her. Peggie Voll - (granddaughter) of Jacob Birdsall has provided some information.

NAME: ENOCH TURLEY

RIG: Pilot Boat

DATE SUNK: November 30, 1843, also reported March 11, 1888

REPORTED POSITION WHERE SUNK: went ashore near Indian River Inlet

MASTER AT TIME OF SINKING: 7 pilots on board (all rescued by Cape Henlopen Life Saving Station)

WEATHER CONDITIONS AT TIME OF SINKING: southeast gale

NAME:	EQUATOR (formerly the U.S.S. Governor Buckingham)
RIG:	Barge (formerly Steam Screw) (formerly hermaphrodite brig)
REGISTERED NUMBER:	7719; Call Letters HGBJ
DATE & LOCATION BUILT:	August 7, 1863; Mystic, Connecticut by Charles Mallory
DATE SUNK:	March 23, 1893
REPORTED POSITION WHERE SUNK:	near Fenwick Island, Maryland
OWNER:	Mallory, Maxon, Fish & Company original owner; Clyde Line, owner
MASTER AT TIME OF SINKING:	4 persons on board (all lost)
CARGO AT TIME OF SINKING:	lumber
HOME PORT:	Philadelphia, Pennsylvania
LAST PORT SAILED FROM:	Norfolk, Virginia
PORT BOUND FOR:	Philadelphia, Pennsylvania
CONSTRUCTION:	959 tons gross; also listed as 1,044 tons gross; wood; 628.09 net tons; length 116.8'; breadth 34.1'; depth 17.5'; 125 h.p.; oak and chestnut; iron and copper fastenings; single screw; one cylinder direct acting engine 36" x 36" one boiler
OTHER DATA:	foundered; sold to U.S. Navy July 29, 1863 for $110,000 and commissioned at New York Navy Yard November 13, 1863; saw service in Civil War; decommissioned March 27, 1865 at Norfolk and sold at public auction at New York July 12, 1865 to J.O. Donohue and sold shortly after to William P. Clyde (Clyde Line) and name changed to EQUATOR; in 1893 she was dismantled and converted to a barge

NAME:	ESTHER ANN
RIG:	Schooner
REGISTERED NUMBER:	206162; Signal Letters LBCD
DATE & LOCATION BUILT:	1909; Bath, Maine by New England Shipbuilding Company., James W. Hawley
DATE SUNK:	October 9, 1920 (also reported as October 11)
REPORTED POSITION WHERE SUNK:	38°21'00"N 74°40'00"W in 108' of water
MASTER AT TIME OF SINKING:	7 man crew
CARGO AT TIME OF SINKING:	coal
HOME PORT:	Hartford, Connecticut
LAST PORT SAILED FROM:	Ramsey
PORT BOUND FOR:	Dublin
CONSTRUCTION:	753 gross tons; 631 net tons; length 181.2'; breadth 37.1'; depth 14.4'; wood; 4 masts
OTHER DATA:	collision with steamship "DUQUESNE"

NAME: EUSTATIA

RIG: Merchantman (ship)

REGISTERED NUMBER: (Dutch)

DATE SUNK: 1664

REPORTED POSITION WHERE SUNK: at anchor off Lewes, Delaware

WEATHER CONDITIONS
AT TIME OF SINKING: whole gale

NAME: H.M.S. FAITHFUL STEWARD

RIG: English Ship

DATE SUNK: September 2, 1785

REPORTED POSITION WHERE SUNK: Rehobeth Beach, Delaware;
                                1/4 mile north of Indian River
                                Inlet; 300 yards off the beach

MASTER AT TIME OF SINKING: Captain William McCasland and
                                360 passengers (200 lost)

CARGO AT TIME OF SINKING: passengers and Irish coins

LAST PORT SAILED FROM: Londonderry, Ireland;
                                July 9, 1785

PORT BOUND FOR: Philadelphia, Pennsylvania

CONSTRUCTION: wood; 350 tons

OTHER DATA: 249 passengers and a cargo of
                                Irish coins; only 68 persons were
                                saved as she wrecked near the
                                Indian River Inlet

Maryland Gazette
September 22, 1785

The following is an account of the unfortunate disaster which befell the ship FAITHFUL STEWARD, Connally McCausland, Master, from Londonderry, bound to this port, taken from a gentleman who was passenger on board:

On the 9th day of July last, said vessel sailed from Londonderry, having on board 249 passengers of respectability, who had with them property to a very considerable amount. They had had a favorable passage, during which nothing of moment occurred, the greatest harmony having prevailed among them, until the night of Thursday the 1st instant, September, when at the hour of 10 o'clock it was thought advisable to try for soundings, and to their great surprise found themselves in four fathoms water, though at dark there was not the smallest appearance of land. The consternation and astonishment which then prevailed, is easier conceived than described, every exertion was used to run the vessel offshore, but in a few minutes she struck the ground, when it was found necessary to cut away her masts and rigging all of which went overboard. On the morning of the 2nd, we found ourselves on Mohobabank, near Indian River, about four leagues to the southward of Cape Henlopen. Every effort was made to save the unhappy sufferers, who remained in the wreck during the night, although distant from the shore only about 100 yards. The same evening she beat to pieces. The sea running extremely high, the boats were with difficulty, disengaged from the wreck, but before they could be manned they drifted ashore, therefore all relief was cut off, except by swimming or getting ashore on pieces of the wreck, and we are sorry to add, that of the above, only 68 persons were saved, among which were the Master, his mates, and 10 seamen. During the course of the day, the inhabitants came down to the beach in numbers, and used every means in their power to relieve the unfortunate people on board among whom were about 100 women and children of whom only 7 were saved. Several persons who escaped from the wreck are since dead from the wounds they received, and others are miserably bruised.

NAME:	FORRESTER
RIG:	Brig
DATE & LOCATION BUILT:	1834; Hampden, Maine
DATE SUNK:	September 16, 1843
REPORTED POSITION WHERE SUNK:	parted both chains and drove ashore near Fenwick Island
MASTER AT TIME OF SINKING:	Captain Berry (all saved)
CARGO AT TIME OF SINKING:	coal
LAST PORT SAILED FROM:	Havre de Grace
PORT BOUND FOR:	New York
WEATHER CONDITIONS AT TIME OF SINKING:	gale on 11th dismasted her off Cape Henlopen and drove her down to Fenwick Island
CONSTRUCTION:	wood; 126 tons
OTHER DATA:	went to pieces at time of beaching

NAME:	FORTUNE
RIG:	Brig
DATE SUNK:	November 29, 1764
REPORTED POSITION WHERE SUNK:	Assateague Beach

NAME: FRANCIS BURRETT

RIG: Schooner

DATE & LOCATION BUILT: Westport, Connecticut; 1853

DATE SUNK: Friday, November 21, 1879

REPORTED POSITION WHERE SUNK: 120 miles southwest of Absecon
                                   Light (possibly in Virginian
                                   waters)

MASTER AT TIME OF SINKING: Captain W. H. Mills, Henry
                                   Brown, mate; Ephraim Mills,
                                   steward; Benjamin Eaton, Edgar
                                   Brown

CARGO AT TIME OF SINKING: pig iron; 170 tons

LAST PORT SAILED FROM: Bangor, Maine

PORT BOUND FOR: Wilmington, Delaware

WEATHER CONDITIONS
AT TIME OF SINKING: gale, heavy seas, snow squalls

CONSTRUCTION: 206 tons

OTHER DATA:

New York Times
November 23, 1879

A Schooner Lost At Sea
The Crew Rescued By The Steamer ANDES

Particulars of the Disaster - The Story as Told by the Captain of the
Abandoned Vessel - The Schooner ANDREW NREINGER Caught in a Gale

The steam-ship ANDES, Capt. Banson, of the Atlas Line, which arrived
from Port au Prince and other West Indian ports yesterday, had on board
the rescued crew of the New York schooner FRANCIS BURRETT, which was
abandoned on the 21st about 120 miles south west of Absecom Light.
Stormy weather was met with by the steamer, and late last Friday morning
she was plowing her way through a heavy sea and against a head wind.
Snow squalls frequently passed over her, and the atmosphere had
partially cleared after one of these when the attention of the second
officer, who was then on the bridge, was attracted to a small vessel,
apparently in distress, about one mile distant on the port beam. The

steam-ship was headed toward the stranger, and in a short time was hove to near by her. The crew of the distressed vessel were eligning to the pumps while the huge waves dashed over her sides. There was but one small piece of canvas set, and the American flag was flying with the union down. The forestop mast was shaking badly, and threatened to fall at any moment. No boat whatever could be discovered on the disabled schooner. It was blowing a gale, and the sea was very heavy and confused. Snow squalls of great violence frequently howled along the uneven surface of the ocean. It was an extremely dangerous task to attempt to rescue the distressed crew, but a life boat was lowered from the Andes, and was successfully launched after it had several times sorrowly escaped being swamped. Her crew sprang into her and rowed away from the steamer under the command of the first officer, Mr. George Steel Hicks. After a hard struggle, she was brought alongside of the lee rail of the Francis Burrett. The latter lurched violently over to leeward at a critical moment and came very near smashing the life-boat and drowning its gallant crew. The officer was obliged to keep off for a moment, and when the schooner was somewhat steadier the boat again came round to the lea side, and when within a short distance of the vessel five men, who were on her deck, caught hold of the ropes which were swinging around wildly in the gale. As she rolled to leeward they were swung out over the life-boat by means of the ropes and dropped into the latter. A small bag of clothing was all that was saved, but the seamen found themselves fortunate in having reached the boat in safety. When they were clear of the wreck they found that a hard struggle lay before them. The wind and sea were against them, and a heavy squall might at any moment capsize the frail boat. Slowly she fought her way back against wind and tide, struggling among the tremendous waves, which threatened to engulf her. At about half an hour past noon she was alongside the steam-ship, and after great difficulty, the crew and the rescued seamen all reached the main deck in safety. The boat was then hauled up to her davits, and the ANDES resumed her voyage and soon left the schooner far astern, drifting helplessly in the trough of the sea, and to all appearances about to sink. In two hours the wreck was out of sight, and the officers of the steam-ship do not think that she kept afloat long after she had been abandoned.

Capt. Mills, of the schooner FRANCIS BURRETT, says he was bound from Bangor, Me., for Wilmington, Del. with a cargo of pig-iron. His vessel had just been thoroughly repaired on the dry-dock, and was thought to be in very good condition. A small portion of her cargo was consigned to this port, and was discharged here last week. The remainder consisted of 170 tons of iron, which was to have been delivered at the works of the Lobdale Car-wheel Company at Wilmington. On Wednesday last the schooner passed Sandy Hook and was proceeding along the Jersey coast on the following morning, when the gale began. She was then being driven fast out to sea by the cold winds which came from the shore. At 3 o'clock in the afternoon all the canvas, with the exception of a small storm trisail was blown away. The seas were heavy, and the iron cargo kept the vessel down low in the water. She labored so violently that a leak was sprung, and the crew were kept constantly at the pumps, while the Captain steered the vessel. It was very difficult for the men to hold their positions owing to the heavy waves which swept the decks. During the night it was found that there were three feet of water in the hold, and the crew were still obliged to keep at work constantly. All the provisions had become entirely spoiled by water, and no one thought of preparing any supper. The pumps were kept going until 3 o'clock on the following morning, the skipper meantime having remained at the wheel. A tremendous sea then almost buried the schooner and washed away her only boat. The water in the hold was gaining slowly but surely, and the prospects of the crew were becoming very gloomy. This condition of affairs lasted until daybreak, when a sharp lookout for sails was begun. At 9 o'clock a barkentine rigged steam-ship sailing north was observed about three miles distant. A signal of distress was hoisted, but the stranger paid no attention to it. Whether she observed the disabled vessel or not could not be discovered. A moment later she was hidden from sight by a furious snow squall, and when the atmosphere became clearer the steamer was nowhere to be seen. The crew were fast becoming exhausted from hard labor and exposure, and this incident greatly discouraged them. When the Andes was first sighted the men were fearful that she, too, would pass them by. When she had changed her course and was approaching they remembered that they had no boat, and there was a great deal of doubt at first about the stranger's willingness to send them a boat. The poor fellows went wild with joy when they observed Officer Hicks and his crew rowing toward them. The gale was so heavy that the ensign, which had been hoisted as a signal of distress, was blown away and a piece of the flag fell into the water near the life boat. When the shipwrecked crew reached the deck of the steamer they were profuse in their thanks to the rescuers. Upon the arrival of the ANDES yesterday the crew of the vessel went on board the schooner H.B. BIRD, of Rockland, which lay at the foot of Twelfth Street. The master of this vessel is a relative of Capt. Mills, and the latter's crew will remain there until to-morrow afternoon, when they will start for their homes. Capt. Mills, who is a stout "down East" old skipper, is very enthusiastic in his praise of Officer Hicks, whom he speaks of as a "British lion". The lost schooner was built at Westport, Conn., in 1853, and registered 206 tons. The names of the crew who so narrowly escaped death are: W. H. Mills of Castine, master; Henry Brown of Belfast, mate; Ephraim Mills, of Rockland, steward; Benjamin Eaton, of Winterport, and Edgar Brown, of Rockland, seamen. The ANDES had a very stormy passage. On the 19th a violent gale from north-east set in, and lasted for 48 hours. The speed of the vessel was slowed down in the meantime.

Copyright 1879/1880/1881/1883/1884/1887/1889/1895/1913/1918 by The New York Times Company. Reprinted by permission.

NAME: **GARLAND**

RIG: Ship

DATE SUNK: April, 1709

REPORTED POSITION WHERE SUNK: Assateague Beach; Lat. 38°20'

CONSTRUCTION: 110 tons

OTHER DATA: 12 survivors

NAME: **GENERAL BERRY**

RIG: Bark

DATE & LOCATION BUILT: 1863; Thomaston, Maine

DATE SUNK: July 10, 1864

REPORTED POSITION WHERE SUNK: 35 miles off Maryland Coast
37°33'N; 74°20'W

OWNER: D. Lord

CARGO AT TIME OF SINKING: 1,116 bales of hay;
36 bales of straw

HOME PORT: Kennebunk, Maine

LAST PORT SAILED FROM: New York

PORT BOUND FOR: Fortress Monroe, Virginia

CONSTRUCTION: wood; 469 tons ? or 1,197 tons ?;
copper and iron fastenings;
2 decks

OTHER DATA: The "C.S.S. FLORIDA", Lt. Charles
M. Morris commanding, burned the
GENERAL BERRY

NAME:	GENERAL MIFFLIN
RIG:	Brig
DATE SUNK:	March, 1777
REPORTED POSITION WHERE SUNK:	Sinepuxent Inlet (on shore)
OWNER:	John Cox and John Chaloner
MASTER AT TIME OF SINKING:	Captain John Hamilton and crew of 90 men
CARGO AT TIME OF SINKING:	prize from English merchantship ELIZABETH
HOME PORT:	Philadelphia, Pennsylvania
LAST PORT SAILED FROM:	Island of Barbados
PORT BOUND FOR:	Philadelphia, Pennsylvania
WEATHER CONDITIONS AT TIME OF SINKING:	storm, snow
CONSTRUCTION:	12 gun privateer
OTHER DATA:	17 men perished attempting to find shelter on the beach

NAME: <u>GEORGE H. BENT</u>

RIG: Schooner

REGISTERED NUMBER: 10836; Call Letters JCFL

DATE & LOCATION BUILT: 1867; Camden, New Jersey

DATE SUNK: December 18, 1888

REPORTED POSITION WHERE SUNK: Delaware Breakwater; 2 miles N x W of Lewes Station

MASTER AT TIME OF SINKING: Captain Scull and 8 crew (all 9 saved)

CARGO AT TIME OF SINKING: railroad ties

HOME PORT: Sommers Point, New Jersey

LAST PORT SAILED FROM: Norfolk, Virginia

PORT BOUND FOR: Philadelphia, Pennsylvania

CONSTRUCTION: wood; 209 tons gross; 198.6 net tons; length 111.0'; breadth 29.0'; depth 8.0'

OTHER DATA: surfboat used to rescue crew

NAME:	GEORGE L. GARLICK
RIG:	Sloop
REGISTERED NUMBER:	85513
DATE & LOCATION BUILT:	1877; Jersey City, New Jersey
DATE SUNK:	November 25, 1889
REPORTED POSITION WHERE SUNK:	point of Cape Henlopen
MASTER AT TIME OF SINKING:	Captain Chamberlain and 1 person (both saved)
HOME PORT:	Sommers Point, New Jersey
LAST PORT SAILED FROM:	Atlantic City, New Jersey
PORT BOUND FOR:	Chincoteaque, Virginia
CONSTRUCTION:	22 tons gross; 21.27 tons net; length 46.5'; breadth 17.0'; depth 5.5'

NAME:	GEORGE G. SIMPSON
RIG:	Steamtug
DATE & LOCATION BUILT:	1882; Camden, New Jersey
DATE SUNK:	March 14, 1888
REPORTED POSITION WHERE SUNK:	steamboat pier at Delaware Breakwater
MASTER AT TIME OF SINKING:	Captain Holt
CONSTRUCTION:	wood; 67' length
OTHER DATA:	See report of LIZZIE CRAWFORD; Mrs. Holt, Mr. Robinson passengers on board

NAME:	GOOD HOPE
RIG:	Ship
DATE SUNK:	October, 1670
REPORTED POSITION WHERE SUNK:	pounded to pieces on beach on Assateague
WEATHER CONDITIONS AT TIME OF SINKING:	storm

NAME:	GORDON C. COOKE (formerly the Lake Louise prior to 1945)
RIG:	Barge (converted by Ford Motor Company in 1927)
REGISTERED NUMBER:	216406; Hull No. 181
DATE & LOCATION BUILT:	June, 1918; Ashtabula, Ohio; launched as War Drum
DATE SUNK:	April 22, 1947
REPORTED POSITION WHERE SUNK:	38°05'25"N 26974.9 X 'C' Loran 74°48'40"W 42173.0 Y
OWNER:	Seaways Transportation Corporation, New York; 1946 to 1947 U.S. Shipping Board, Boston, Massachusetts; 1918 to 1927 Ford Motor Company, Detroit, Michigan; 1927 to 1943 U.S. War Shipping Administration, Washington, DC; 1943 to 1946
MASTER AT TIME OF SINKING:	(crew of 10)
CARGO AT TIME OF SINKING:	freight and gypsum rock
HOME PORT:	New York City
PHOTOGRAPH &/OR DRAWING:	Center for Archival Collections Bowling Green State University Bowling Green, Ohio 43403
CONSTRUCTION:	2,023 gross tons; 1,890 net tons; length 253.5'; width 43.5'; depth 22.5'; no engine
OTHER DATA:	sunk as a result of collision with "HARFORD" while COOKE was in tow of "BARLOW"; in 105' of water

GORDON C. COOKE (LAKE LOUISE)
Photo courtesy of the Institute for Great Lakes Research,
Bowling Green State University

NAME:	<u>GOVERNOR JACKSON</u>
RIG:	Schooner-Barge
REGISTERED NUMBER:	86000
DATE & LOCATION BUILT:	1865; Miramichi, N.S.
DATE SUNK:	August 22, 1888
REPORTED POSITION WHERE SUNK:	20 miles E.N.E. (67°30'E) of Winter Quarter Shoal
CARGO AT TIME OF SINKING:	coal
HOME PORT:	Baltimore, Maryland
LAST PORT SAILED FROM:	Newport News, Virginia
PORT BOUND FOR:	Providence, Rhode Island
CONSTRUCTION:	515.24 gross tons; 493.70 net tons; hull planking 3-1/2" thick; deck planks 3"; planking bolts 12/16" diameter; anchor chain 1-7/16" diameter; length 143.0'; depth 18.6'; breadth 28.7'
OTHER DATA:	3 lives lost

NAME: **GREYHOUND**

RIG: Man of War (Spanish)

DATE SUNK: 1750 (August)

REPORTED POSITION WHERE SUNK: ashore at Matchapungo Shoals

MASTER AT TIME OF SINKING: Captain Onness (Irishman) (4 lost) also 20 English prisoners

CARGO AT TIME OF SINKING: Spanish snuff; Spanish tobacco; Mohogany; money

LAST PORT SAILED FROM: Havana, Cuba

WEATHER CONDITIONS AT TIME OF SINKING: gale

CONSTRUCTION: 50 guns

OTHER DATA: 22 pieces of "8" have been washed ashore near Assateaque bearing dates from 1733 to 1740

"MARYLAND GAZZETTE"
Wednesday, September 12, 1750

NAME: **GUERNSEY**

RIG: Snow

DATE SUNK: September 13, 1734

REPORTED POSITION WHERE SUNK: Assateague Beach

OTHER DATA: grounded

Snow

NAME:	GYPSUM PRINCE
RIG:	Steam Screw
REGISTERED NUMBER:	British 147789; Call Signal GNCM
DATE & LOCATION BUILT:	1927; Furness Shipbuilding Company, Ltd., Haverton Hill on Tees
DATE SUNK:	March 4, 1942 at 6:45 a.m.
REPORTED POSITION WHERE SUNK:	3-1/2 miles off Lewes
EXACT POSITION:	38°48'15"N 1.2 miles, 117 from light on south end of rock breakwater 75°04'10"W 1.1 miles off tip of Cape Henlopen, Delaware
OWNER:	Gypsum Packet Company, Ltd.
MASTER AT TIME OF SINKING:	Captain Owen Jones
HOME PORT:	Middlesborough
LAST PORT SAILED FROM:	Digby
PORT BOUND FOR:	Philadelphia
PHOTOGRAPH &/OR DRAWING:	Photograph No. 4505, Courtesy Steamship Historical Society of U.S.A.
CONSTRUCTION:	Lloyds Register Class +10041; 3,915 gross tons; length 347'8"; breadth 52'8"; depth 23"
OTHER DATA:	Captain and 6 crewmen lost; total of 26 aboard; collision with S.S. VOCO; the starboard bow of the S.S. VOCO was damaged by the collision; wreck was cleared to a depth of 50'
	See also New York Times article March 4, 1942

New York Times
March 4, 1942

FREIGHTER IS SUNK IN COAST COLLISION

GYPSUM PRINCE and the Tanker, VOCO, Both British, Crash Off Delaware
Latter Damaged - 6 Men Lost, 20 Rescued - Master of Cargo Ship Drowned
Both Vessels Running Dark Because of Submarines

LEWES, Del., March 4 - The 3,915-ton British freighter GYPSUM PRINCE was sunk three and a half miles off this port early this morning after a collision with the British tanker VOCO of 5,090 tons. Six members of the crew of the GYPSUM PRINCE, including her master, Captain Owen Jones, lost their lives and twenty others were rescued by the Coast Guard.

Both ships were sailing without lights because of the submarine danger. The accident occurred at 6:15 a.m. while the visibility was still bad. The GYPSUM PRINCE was bound in for the port of Philadelphia, while the VOCO was outwardbound for an undisclosed port.

Captain Robert W. Blair of Kendall, England, master of the VOCO, said that he first sighted the GYPSUM PRINCE when she was about two miles distant and that he sounded a passing signal, which was not acknowledged by the other vessel until she was barely half a mile away. Captain Blair said that he sensed that a collision was imminent and called for full speed astern, but the ships crashed despite his efforts.

Six of the crew of the GYPSUM PRINCE, including a father and son, Harry O'Neil, 55 years old, and Garfield O'Neil, 29, both of Nova Scotia, were rescued from the top of a capsized lifeboat after it had drifted some distance. The elder O'Neil said that he and John McAllister, chief steward, had seen Captain Jones struggling in the water and had tried to pull him on top of the overturned boat.

"The sea was too rough," O'Neil said, "and the captain slipped away from us."

Captain Jones' body floated ashore later in the morning, as did those of Harry Wood, chief cook, and Jake Kilcup, ordinary seaman, of the GYPSUM PRINCE. Three other members of the crew missing and presumably lost were Walter Morgan, first mate; John Parsons, radio operator; and Matthew Olson, able-bodied seaman.

There were no casualties aboard the VOCO, which put back into the Delaware Bay with a big hole in the starboard bow.

Copyright 1920/1927/* by The New York Times Company
Reprinted by permission.

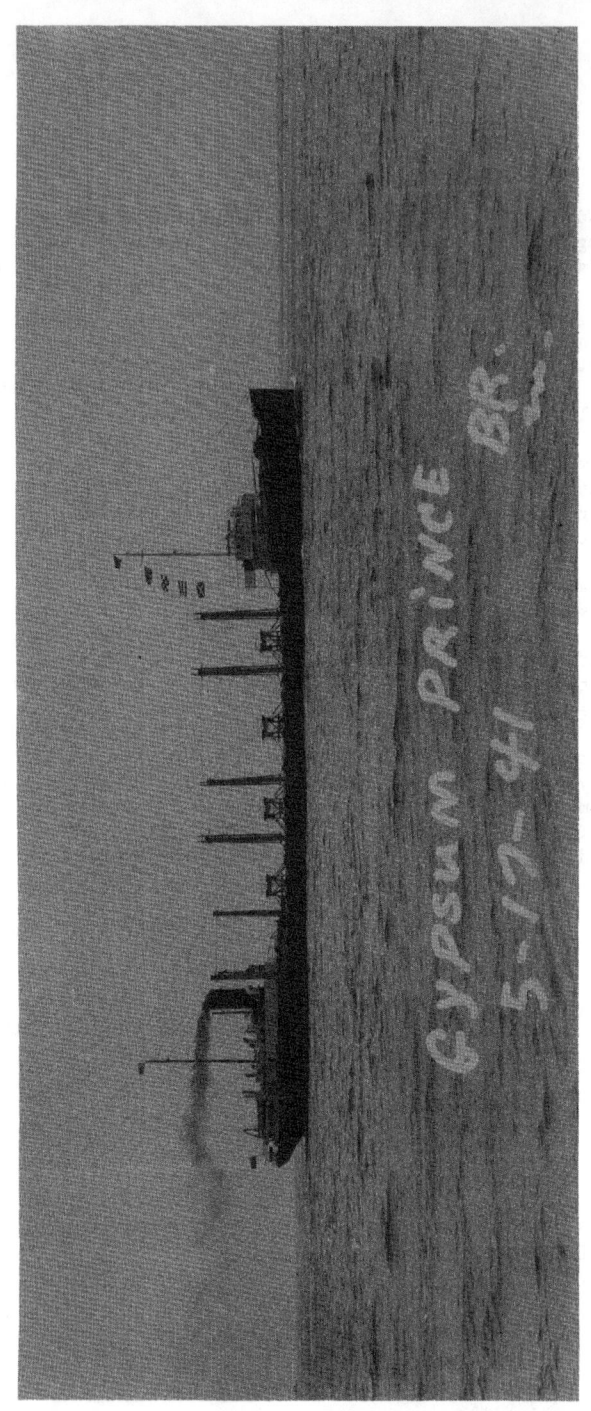

GYPSUM PRINCE
Courtesy of the Steamship Historical Society Collection,
University of Baltimore Library

NAME:	<u>HANNAH A. LENNEN</u>
RIG:	Steam Screw
REGISTERED NUMBER:	96542
DATE & LOCATION BUILT:	1901
DATE SUNK:	June 16, 1944
REPORTED POSITION WHERE SUNK:	harbor end of entrance to Delaware Bay 38° 50'31"N 74° 55'58"W
CONSTRUCTION:	136 tons
OTHER DATA:	collision with oil tanker "Beuna Vista"

NAME:	<u>HAPPY RETURN</u>
RIG:	Snow
DATE SUNK:	October 1, 1747
REPORTED POSITION WHERE SUNK:	grounded on Hen and Chicken Shoal, Delaware, and went to pieces
MASTER AT TIME OF SINKING:	Captain Scott
CARGO AT TIME OF SINKING:	servants (50 drowned)
LAST PORT SAILED FROM:	Londonberry
PORT BOUND FOR:	Philadelphia

NAME:	**HARRISBURG**
RIG:	Schooner
DATE SUNK:	September 13, 1846
REPORTED POSITION WHERE SUNK:	4 miles south of Lewes, Delaware on beach
HOME PORT:	Elizabethport
LAST PORT SAILED FROM:	New York
PORT BOUND FOR:	Philadelphia
WEATHER CONDITIONS AT TIME OF SINKING:	gale
OTHER DATA:	captain and crew believed lost

NAME:	**HARRY K. FOOKS**
RIG:	Oil Screw (fishing service)
REGISTERED NUMBER:	221418
DATE & LOCATION BUILT:	1921; Vinyard Shipbuilding Company; Milford, Delaware
DATE SUNK:	September 10, 1941
REPORTED POSITION WHERE SUNK:	1,000 yards from Hens & Chickens whistle bouy N 38°42'36" W 74°59'48" in 33' of water
OWNER:	Menhaden Products Company or Edwards Company, Reedville, Virginia
PHOTOGRAPH &/OR DRAWING:	Mariners Museum Drawing CN 1122 (lines taken from half model)
CONSTRUCTION:	wood; 184 tons; length 118.5'; breadth 21.9'; depth; 9.9'; 500 h.p. engine
OTHER DATA:	15 man crew; collision with steamship E.J. CODD

NAME: HENRY & CHARLES

RIG: Ship (American)

DATE SUNK: 1796

NAME: HERCULES

RIG: Barge

REGISTERED NUMBER: 42743

DATE & LOCATION BUILT: 1894; Brooklyn, New York

DATE SUNK: January 19, 1901

REPORTED POSITION WHERE SUNK: 1/2 mile west of the point of Cape Henlopen

HOME PORT: Philadelphia, Pennsylvania

LAST PORT SAILED FROM: Philadelphia, Pennsylvania

PORT BOUND FOR: Delaware Breakwater

CONSTRUCTION: 149 tons gross; 141 tons net

NAME: HESPER

RIG: Gas Screw

DATE SUNK: April 30, 1919

REPORTED POSITION WHERE SUNK: Delaware Capes

NAME: **HVSOLEF**

RIG: Steam Screw

REGISTERED NUMBER: 25490 (Lloyd's Registry)

DATE & LOCATION BUILT: 1927

DATE SUNK: March 10, 1942

REPORTED POSITION WHERE SUNK: 2 miles east of Fenwick Island Light Buoy
38°28'57"N; 74°32'39"W
Old Loran: 3H4 3329
            3H5 3077

CARGO AT TIME OF SINKING: sugar

LAST PORT SAILED FROM: Cuba

PORT BOUND FOR: Boston

WEATHER CONDITIONS
AT TIME OF SINKING: clear, sea slight chop

PHOTOGRAPH &/OR DRAWING: Mariners Museum Photo No. PB8118

CONSTRUCTION: steel; 1,630 gross tons; 255' long; 35.5' beam

OTHER DATA: The vessel was cruising at 13 knots when she was struck on the starboard side near the No. 3 hatch by a torpedo from a German submarine. A second torpedo hit amidships. The ship sank in less than 2 minutes. Of the 20 person crew, 14 survivors came ashore at Fenwick Island. Wreck lays in 130' to 140' of water on a sand bottom. The forward section of the wreck is very low and upright but boilers and other parts of ship extend off the sand 25 feet. The stern is gone.

Courtesy of the Mariners Museum, Newport News, Virginia 23606

NAME:	**IL SALVATORE**
RIG:	Brig
REPORTED POSITION WHERE SUNK:	wrecked against iron pier 1 mile east of Lewes Station
CARGO AT TIME OF SINKING:	oil
HOME PORT:	Naples, Italy
LAST PORT SAILED FROM:	Philadelphia, Pennsylvania
PORT BOUND FOR:	Cagliari, Italy

NAME:	**IRA D. STURGIS**
RIG:	Schooner
REGISTERED NUMBER:	100062
DATE & LOCATION BUILT:	1873; Bath, Maine
DATE SUNK:	February 15, 1906
REPORTED POSITION WHERE SUNK:	1-1/2 miles north of Indian River Inlet Life Saving Station; 3-1/2 miles south of Rehobeth Beach Life Saving Station; 150 yards from beach
OWNER:	H. P. Havens in 1906
MASTER AT TIME OF SINKING:	E. L. Crammer & 5 crewmen (all 6 saved)
CARGO AT TIME OF SINKING:	pinewood
HOME PORT:	New York
LAST PORT SAILED FROM:	James River, Virginia
PORT BOUND FOR:	New York
WEATHER CONDITIONS AT TIME OF SINKING:	N.N.W. wind; strong; rough seas
CONSTRUCTION:	3 masts; 235 tons; length 118.3'; breadth 30'; depth 8.5'; wood with iron and copper fastenings; centerboard tern

NAME:	U.S.S. JACOB JONES
RIG:	Destroyer
REGISTERED NUMBER:	DD-130
DATE & LOCATION BUILT:	1918 (commissioned in 1919)
DATE SUNK:	February 28, 1942 at 5 a.m. by the German submarine U-578 using 3 torpedoes; one hit just aft of the bridge; another hit 40' forward of the fantail
REPORTED POSITION WHERE SUNK:	30 miles east of Cape Henlopen; wreck is in two pieces: stern section 38°37'10"N 74°23'12"W; main section 38°40'15"N 74°28'40"W or 38°38'15"N 74°23'58"W
MASTER AT TIME OF SINKING:	Lieutenant Commander Hugh David Black of Oradell, New Jersey; Executive Officer Lieutenant Commander Thomas W. Marshall, Jr.; 12 men were rescued; about 120 were lost including all officers.
CARGO AT TIME OF SINKING:	none
HOME PORT:	New York City
LAST PORT SAILED FROM:	New York City
PORT BOUND FOR:	Atlantic submarine patrol
WEATHER CONDITIONS AT TIME OF SINKING:	fair; calm seas; 38°F.
PHOTOGRAPH &/OR DRAWING:	Mariners Museum Photo - The Stone Collection
CONSTRUCTION:	steel; length 314'4"; beam 30'6"; draft 12'4"; 4" guns; 12 torpedo tubes; top speed 35 knots.

OTHER DATA: As of 1977, wreck is in 2 pieces. Section with boiler room lays on clean sand bottom in 110' of water and extends up off the bottom about 30' and is upright; lot of brass valves and hardware in this section; usually good visibility about 25' to 35'. Charter boat Captains out of Ocean City, Maryland and Indian River Inlet, Delaware know exact location.

The New York Times
Wednesday, March 4, 1942

U-Boat Sinks U.S. Destroyer Off Cape May; All But 11 Lost

Just before dawn last Saturday, the United States destroyer JACOB JONES, a 1,090-ton craft dating back to the first World War, was torpedoed and sunk by an enemy submarine off Cape May, N.J., it was announced yesterday. Only eleven enlisted men were saved. The Navy did not disclose the exact number lost, but the normal complement of a ship of this type is about seven officers and 125 to 150 enlisted men.

As the Navy was revealing this tragedy yesterday, word came from Puerto Rico that another Axis submarine had fired the first shots to land on United States soil from Atlantic waters since the war began. Thirty shells burst against the steep cliffs of Mona Island Monday evening, according to The Associated Press, but caused no damage or casualties on this tiny fishing resort, fifty miles southwest of Puerto Rico.

First Navy Ship Loss Here

The JACOB JONES was the first naval vessel known to have been lost in our Atlantic coastal waters since the war began, although the sinking of twenty-four merchant ships and the damaging of three others in this area have been disclosed by the Navy. She was the fourteenth ship lost by the Navy in all areas, including the destroyer Reuben James, sent to the bottom before formal hostilities began.

The eleven survivors of the JACOB JONES - nine engine room ratings and two apprentice seamen - were picked up after drifting for four hours on the life rafts in a rough sea and were landed at Cape May, where they were permitted yesterday to tell their stories. Because all of them were below deck at the time, they could give only scanty information about the sinking, but they attested to the calm courage with which the ordeal was met.

This is an account of two survivors: Joseph Paul Tidwell of Tuscaloosa, Alabama, and Thomas R. Moody of Franklin, Kentucky.

This first torpedo hit the JACOB JONES' bow at 4:55 a.m., wrecking the bridge and forward living areas and killing the captain, Lieutenant Commander Hugh David Black, her executive officer Lieutenant Commander Thomas W. Marshall, Jr., and many of the enlisted men asleep in the forward compartments. Less than one minute later, the 2nd torpedo struck the stern wrecking that section and exploding some of the depth charges carried on racks there ready for use. These explosions also killed some of the men already in the oil coated water. Just about all the survivors were from the amidship section which stayed afloat for almost an hour allowing the few men left alive time to don extra heavy underwear and drink hot coffee.

Tidwell was probably the only survivor who actually saw the submarine outlined in the darkness 100 yards off the port side. He had just taken a break from his duty in the aft engine room to get sugar for his coffee from the galley when a tremendous explosion forward bogged the destroyer down. Everything in the galley was flying everywhere when the second explosion came. Tidwell rushed out on deck to find some of the men cutting away the life rafts and jumping into the water. "I jumped in the water and climbed on one raft with Struthers and Dors. There was fuel oil in the water all around, but it did not catch fire," he stated and added that all through the period of abandoning ship the men were calm and collected. The life raft tossed about in the choppy water bumping into debris, so that the three men on the raft, Tidwell, Dors, and Struthers decided that one of them would have to get off. Dors got off the raft, and climbed back aboard the remaining mid-section of the destroyer to get another raft, but could not break one loose. He remained on board until the water was up to his feet. Dors jumped into the sea again and swam for another raft. Soon after the mid-section of the ship disappeared beneath the waves, another explosion shot up from out of the water, knocking some of the men off the rafts.

Thomas Moody also had been in the after engine room when the firt torpedo hit, grabbing his coat and life jacket and rushing topside where he immediately tried to launch a life boat, but found the launching equipment had been smashed. He then made his way to the galley to look for some coffee. "I wasn't going to go out in that cold water without getting something warm in my stomach!" Moody and another fellow, George Pantall, found a locker full of heavy underwear and started passing it out amongst some of the men. They went out on deck to cut three life rafts loose, hurling them over the side to the men struggling in the water. Moody tried to make a raft for himself out of two gasoline drums but abandoned the effort as the ship was settling too fast. "I jumped over the side and swam around until I found a raft. Just as I grabbed hold, an explosion went off in the ship. I was blown clear of the water. I finally got back on the raft. I was the thirteenth man to get on it. After I got on it we pulled Pantall over the side."

Copyright 1920/1927/* by The New York Times Company
Reprinted by permission.

The raft measured only 5' x 9', but the men found room on it. Only Pantall, Moody, Louis Hollenbeck, and Richard Dors were able to hang on until they were picked up four hours later.

The German submarine that sank the JACOB JONES was U-578 commanded by Captain E.A. Rehwinkel. The sub was a type VIII C built by Blohm and Voss in Hamburg and launched May 15, 1941. She carried 49 men and was lost with all hands including Captain Rehwinkel on August 10, 1942, northwest of Cape Ortegal, Spain, by a bombing attack.

The following has been translated from Captain Rehwinkel's "war diary":

Time 1025 (European time - American time would be about 4:25 a.m.) "To starboard - a ship with no light. Reciprical course. I change to parallel course."

Time 1029 "Readiness for action" my order. "I go a little in front of him because I like to attack above water. My position is very good. Behind me is a very dark horizon. Moon still shines. One hour before sunrise, most behind light clouds. Visability good but there is still haziness. "Torpedo 1, 3, and 5 are clear." Gradually I get the impression that it is a typical cruiser silhouette. Details are at this moment not distinguishable.

Time 1050 "Turn to course 230 . Ready to attack. Deep 3 meters, comply with the aim. I forced the attack because in two hours it will be bright daylight and I want to disappear into deeper water. We are now very close to the cruiser. We are in a very good position. We are surprised they do not see us."

Time 1057 "Two torpedos on attack course 240 , ready to fire. Right after we fired, we had some doubt if it really was a cruiser. Because we had the light against us it was very difficult to recognize details of the ship at this time. Now we believe it is a destroyer. We see now it has 4 smokestacks. We were now so close we had no more time to decide what exactly it is. The first direct hit was near the center, followed by a strong explosion and thick black oil smoke. The second direct hit was in the afterdeck, followed by 9 very strong detonations like from WABO or mines. Also, our ship is shaking and we had some trouble with our electricity. There was no defense. Through the smoke we passed the sinking ship."

Korvettenkapitan E.A. Rehwinkel

Photostat of Captain Rehwinkel's War Diary:

Vorkommnisse M 18412

Geheime Kommandosache Prüf.Nr.: 4

Kriegstagebuch
des
Unterseebootes "U 578"

Kommandant: Korv.Kapt. Rehwinkel

Angefangen am: 29. Januar 1942
Beendet am: 25. März 1942

Anlagen:

1 Wegekarte für Prüf.Nr.	1 - 5
Auszug aus der Funkkladde M.Allg.	2 - 4
5 Torpedeschußmeldungen für Prüf.Nr.	1 - 2
2 Gefechtsskizzen für Prüf.Nr.	1
Funkkladde M Allgemein " "	1
Funkkladde M Offisier " "	1

Verteiler:

7. U.- Flottille	Prüf.Nr.	1
Befehlshaber der Unterseeboote	" "	2
2. Admiral der Unterseeboote	" "	3
Oberkommando der Kriegsmarine	" "	4+5

Anlage 282 zu 1/Skl 11905/42 Gkdos.

B. 36. Kriegstagebuch.   Din A 3

Block-Nr. 4655   **Schußmeldung**   Seite: 9
für Überwasserstreitkräfte und U-Boote

U. 578   **Geheim!**   Leutnant z.S. Tiesler, I.W.O.
(Schießendes Fahrzeug)   (Dienstgrad, Name und Dienststellung des Schützen)

Datum: 28. Febr. 1942 Ort: ☐ CA 5458 Uhrzeit des Schusses: 1057ʰ

Wassertiefe: 24 m Wetter: teilweise bedeckt Sicht gut, Mondschein Wind: NW.3

Seegang: 2   Dünung: Richtung u. Stärke keine Dünung

Ziel: 4=Schornstein=Zerstörer   94 m   2,6 m
Typ nicht genau zu bestimmen (Größe) (Länge) (Tiefgang)

Beladezustand u. Ladung: ./.

Erfolg: 2 Treffer / ..... Fehlschuß. Angriffsschuß ~~Fangschuß~~ (auf gestopptliegendes Ziel)

Lfd. Nr.		~~Einzelschuß~~, ~~Doppelschuß~~ Fächerschuß	1	2	3	4
1		Zeittakt in sec und Streuwinkel in Graden	2,5sec 3 Grad			
2	Torpedo	Art, Nummer, Aptierung	20605 G 7e	26343 G 7e		
3		V_t und eingestellte Laufstrecke	30sm/h 120hm	30sm/h 120 hm		
4		Eingestellte Tiefe	3	3		
5	Pi	Nummer, Art der Aptierung	9738	9163		
6		~~Bezeichnung~~	Pi.G 7a AZ FS rot			
7		S-Einstellring				
8	Rohr	Bezeichnung	I	III		
9		Ausstoßart	ohne	Kolben		
10	Beim Schuß	Eigene Fahrt	7 sm/h			
11		Eigener Kurs	240°			
12		Schiffspeilung	1,5°			
13		Schußwinkel	25°			
14		Zielstelle, Ziel- und Rechengerät	Brücke, Zieloptik mit T.Vh-R.			
15		Abkommpunkt	Achterkante 2. Schornstein			
16		Torpedokurs	264,5°	261,5°		
17		Eingestellte Schußunterlagen	V_g = 12 sm/h	V_{gr}.65° grün 20°		
18		Tauchtiefe beim Schuß (nur bei U-Booten)	über Wasser			
19		Lastigkeit beim Schuß (bei Schiffen usw. Krängung beim Schuß)	0°	0°		
20		Entfernung beim Schuß u. beob. Laufzeit	525m 34sec			
21		Torpedoniedergang und Lauf				
22		Schuß im Abdrehen oder auf geraden Kurs	auf geradem Kurs			
23		Eingestellter Winkel nach Farbe u. Graden	~~24,5°~~ 24,5°	~~24,0°~~ 21,5°		
24		Bei G7e und Schußweite über 3000 m: a) letzte Nachladung vor dem Schuß:	21.2.	23.2.		

- 13 -

Datum und Uhrzeit	Angabe des Ortes, Wind, Wetter, Seegang, Beleuchtung, Sichtigkeit der Luft, Mondschein usw.	Vorkommnisse
0834	CA 5217 Wetter unverändert	Eutzangriff auf Kurs 234 Gfrad E = 2500 m. Einzelschuß aus dem inzwischen nachgeladenen Rohr I, geht vorbei. (Gefechtsskizze siehe Torp.Schußmeldungen) Auch im diesem Falle folge ich dem anscheinend zu langsam geschätzten Schiffe nicht. Das Vorsetzen würde bei den Sichtverhältnissen zuviel Brennstoff kosten und mich bis zum Beginn der Helligkeit in die Nähe von New York bringen. unter/ Absicht: Tagsüberwasser innerhalb der 50 m Linie und bei Beginn der Dunkelheit wieder in der Nähe der 20 m Linie nördl. Five Fathom Bank F'schiff zu stehhn. sind
1100		Südöstl. Kurse. Rohre nachgeladen.
1200	CA 5274, NW 3, See 2, gute Sicht, fast wolkenlos.	Etmal: N.W. 119,3 sm, u.W. 27,9 sm.
1245		Es wird hell. Getaucht zum Unterwassermarsch mit südl. u. westl. Kursen.
1600	CA 5279,	
2000	CA 5521	
2400	CA 5433	...Reluuuulol...
28.2. 0105	WNW 2-3, See 2, leichter Dunst, heller Mondschein, zieml. gute Sicht.	Aufgetaucht. Mit Kurs 270 Grad auf die 20 m Linie zumarschiert. Ausweichen vor mehreren Fischern.
0240		Kurs 210 Grad.
0400	CA 5432, NW 3, See 2, sonst unverändert.	
0800	CA 5456,	
0810		Bb. voraus hell beleuchteter Dampfer mit nördl. Kurs in Sicht. Es ist ein Schwede, wahrscheinlich "Gullmaren". Ich halte gut frei von ihm.
0900		Kurs 180 Grad.
1025		Stb. voraus abgeblendetes Fahrzeug in Sicht mit ungefährem Gegenkurs. Aufgedreht zum Parallelkurs.
1029		"Auf Gefechtsstationen". Ich setze mich vor, um ü.W. anzugreifen. Stehe günstig vor dunklem Horizont im Osten. Mond steht - eine Stunden vor Untergang - meist hinter leichten Wolken. Beleuchtung ist gut, aber etwas verschwommen. Rohr I,III und V klar. Allmählich habe ich den Eindruck einer typischen Kreuzersilhouette. Um Einzelheiten zu unterscheiden, ist die Lage noch zu spitz.

- 15 -

Datum und Uhrzeit	Angabe des Ortes, Wind, Wetter, Seegang, Beleuchtung, Sichtigkeit der Luft, Mondschein usw.	Vorkommnisse
		Das wären also fast 900 m Schuß-E gewesen, wodurch ich in meiner Ansicht bestärkt wurde. Tatsächlich waren es aber nur 34 sec., also etwa 500 m, die schließlich mehr wiegen als alle Wunschbeobachtungen.
1200	CA 5494	Etmal: Ü.W. 85,5 sm, u.W. 24 sm.
1236		2 Detonationen weit weg.
1305	Morgendämmerung	Getaucht zum Unterwassermarsch.
1600	CA 5811	Zwischen 1700 und 1900 Uhr gelegentlich Detonation, sehr weit weg.
1935	NW 4, See 4, einzelne Wolken, Sonne, sehr gute Sicht.	Aufgetaucht zum Durchlüften.
1954		Getaucht. Kurs 90 Grad.
2000	CA 5815	
2230		2 Wabo., davon die letzte etwas näher. Gleichzeitig Meldung von Horchraum, daß S-Gerät gehört wird. Es hat die Klangfarbe wie etwa unser Tonlot. Man hört in gleichmäßigen Intervallen 2 Tonschläge.
		Wir sind noch nicht auf tiefen Wasser, daher Schleichfahrt.
		Nach einiger Zeit ändern sich die Geräusche. Schließlich wird fast überall etwas gehört. Ich glaube, die Hörcher sind allmählich etwas nervös geworden. Sicher haben wir nach dem Hochgehen der 9 Wabos in unmittelbarer Nähe nun auch einige Eigengeräusche mehr. Ich bleibe aber noch unten, weil ich mit starker Luftaufklärung bei Tage rechne.
2400	CA 5824	......Schmuckel......
1.3. 0130	Es ist fast dunkel.	Aufgetaucht. Kurs 90 Grad, später 80 Grad (Scheinkurse). Beide Masch. L.F. (Ladung)
0241		Funkspruch: 1.) 27.2. Qu. CA 5211 vollen Tanker 10 000 Brt. Treffer Mitte. Nach Explosion zusammenknickend und sofort überall brennend. Später 2. Explosion. Sonst keine Beobachtungen, da abgedrängt. Halte Totalverlust für sicher. Zweierfächer und Einzelschuß auf weitere Schiffe fehl. 28.2. Qu. CA 5458 Kriegsschiff mit 4 Schornsteinen mit Zweierfächer versenkt. Zweifel, 'Ob Typ "Memphis" oder Zerstörer. Letzteres unwahrscheinlich wegen Torpedotiefe 3 m. Nach Treffer Mitte sofort starke Explosion und Ölqualmwolke, nach Treffer achtern 9 Detonationen wie Wabo.

Anlaufskizze mit Schußbild. Wie sind Schußunterlagen erworben? Besondere Beobachtungen. Abwehr Erklärung für Fehlschuß:

Schußunterlagen wurden ausgedampft. Keine Abwehr.

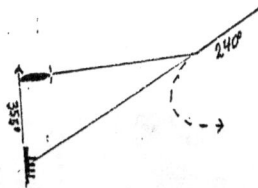

Wirkung am Ziel. Höhe und Aussehen der Sprengsäule. Zeit bis zum vollkommenen Untergang. Wahrnehmungen im eigenen Boot:

1. Treffer Mitte, starke Explosion und dicker Ölqualm. 2. Treffer am Heck, darauffolgende 9 Wabodetonationen. Zuletzt brennende Teile beobachtet anscheinend ragen Wrackteile wegen geringer Wassertiefe an die Oberfläche.

Lt.z.S.u.I.W.O.   Korv.Kpt.u.Kmdt.
Unterschrift des Schutzen - Unterschrift des Kmdten. - gegebf. beglaubigt.

Courtesy of the Mariners Museum, Newport News, Virginia 23606

NAME:	JAMES R. MARKS
RIG:	Sloop
DATE SUNK:	September 10, 1846
REPORTED POSITION WHERE SUNK:	on beach 2 miles south of Cape Henlopen
MASTER AT TIME OF SINKING:	Captain Robbins of Indian River
LAST PORT SAILED FROM:	Norwich
PORT BOUND FOR:	Philadelphia
OTHER DATA:	total loss

NAME:	J. HENRY EDMONDS
RIG:	Gas Screw (aux. Schooner) (Pilot Boat)
REGISTERED NUMBER:	77078
DATE & LOCATION BUILT:	1893
DATE SUNK:	March 13, 1928; 4:22 p.m.
REPORTED POSITION WHERE SUNK:	stranded at Cape Henlopen east of radio station; vessel passed Overfalls Light bearing southeast about 1-1/2 miles and steering west making 7-1/2 knots at 4:20 p.m.; ran hard aground at 4:22 p.m.
OWNER:	Pilots Association for the Bay & River Delaware (Solomon Bettler signed report)
MASTER AT TIME OF SINKING:	Captain Larus Rodreth of Lewes, Delaware and 8 persons
HOME PORT:	Wilmington, Delaware
LAST PORT SAILED FROM:	Cape May, New Jersey
PORT BOUND FOR:	Delaware breakwater
WEATHER CONDITIONS AT TIME OF SINKING:	fog; moderate breeze
CONSTRUCTION:	wood; 72 tons

NAME:	JAMES DUFFIELD
RIG:	Schooner
REGISTERED NUMBER:	American 76849; Call Letters KGQV
DATE & LOCATION BUILT:	1889; New London, Connecticut
DATE SUNK:	April 30, 1912
REPORTED POSITION WHERE SUNK:	at Cape Henlopen
OWNER:	James Davidson & Son
CARGO AT TIME OF SINKING:	stone
HOME PORT:	Hartford, Connecticut
LAST PORT SAILED FROM:	Portland, Connecticut
PORT BOUND FOR:	Philadelphia, Pennsylvania
CONSTRUCTION:	wood; 3 masts; 178 net tons; 187 gross tons; length 112.3'; breadth 28.0'; depth 8.8'

NAME:	JAN MELCHERS (ex. Stephen J. Melchers; ex. Chandos)
RIG:	Ship
DATE & LOCATION BUILT:	October, 1869; Belfast, Maine
DATE SUNK:	May 2, 1888
REPORTED POSITION WHERE SUNK:	near Fenwick Island Shoal
OWNER:	S. J. Melchers
HOME PORT:	Schiedam, Holland
CONSTRUCTION:	white oak; yellow pine; iron and copper fastenings; sheathed with yellow metal; length 121'; beam 38'; depth 25.9'; 1,448 tons
OTHER DATA:	foundered

NAME:	J. D. ROBINSON
RIG:	Schooner
REGISTERED NUMBER:	75689; Call Letters JQLN
DATE & LOCATION BUILT:	1874 by Chas. Minott in Phippsburg yard at Bath, Maine
DATE SUNK:	September 10, 1889
REPORTED POSITION WHERE SUNK:	200 yards west of Lewes Station broadside to a bar
MASTER AT TIME OF SINKING:	Captain Hogan and 7 persons (all 8 saved by Lewes Station)
CARGO AT TIME OF SINKING:	coal - some saved
HOME PORT:	Bath, Maine
LAST PORT SAILED FROM:	Philadelphia, Pennsylvania
PORT BOUND FOR:	Portland, Maine
CONSTRUCTION:	471 tons; length 135.9'; breadth 30.9'; depth 15.9'; 447.30 net tons
OTHER DATA:	total loss

NAME:	JOHN
RIG:	Ship
REGISTERED NUMBER:	American
DATE & LOCATION BUILT:	1795; Salem, Massachusetts
DATE SUNK:	1797
MASTER AT TIME OF SINKING:	Captain Folger

NAME: JOHN J. WARD

RIG: Schooner
REGISTERED NUMBER: 13827; Call Letters JDNK
DATE & LOCATION BUILT: 1867; East Newark, New Jersey
DATE SUNK: March 5, 1907
REPORTED POSITION WHERE SUNK: Delaware Breakwater
CARGO AT TIME OF SINKING: Ballast
HOME PORT: New York
LAST PORT SAILED FROM: New York
PORT BOUND FOR: James River
CONSTRUCTION: 3 masts; wood; 280 tons net;
                                   295 gross tons; length 127.0';
                                   breadth 30.2'; depth 10.1'
OTHER DATA: stranded

NAME: JOHN McMAKIN

RIG: Sternwheel Steamer
DATE & LOCATION BUILT: 1853; Philadelphia, Pennsylvania
DATE SUNK: August, 1860
REPORTED POSITION WHERE SUNK: Lewes, Delaware
HOME PORT: Lamberton, New Jersey
CONSTRUCTION: 158 tons
OTHER DATA: burned

NAME:	JOHN PROCTOR
RIG:	Schooner
REGISTERED NUMBER:	75567; Call Letters JNLG
DATE & LOCATION BUILT:	1873; Weldoboro, Maine
DATE SUNK:	September 13, 1909 (also reported as January 2, 1879)
REPORTED POSITION WHERE SUNK:	Cape Henlopen area 25 miles southeast of Sandy Hook, New Jersey (2 lost)
CARGO AT TIME OF SINKING:	ballast
HOME PORT:	Boston, Massachusetts
LAST PORT SAILED FROM:	Boston, Massachusetts
PORT BOUND FOR:	Baltimore, Maryland
PHOTOGRAPH &/OR DRAWING:	Delaware State Archives SH 263P
CONSTRUCTION:	498 tons; 455 net tons; wood; 3 masts; length 180.0'; breadth 32.0'; depth 15.6'

Courtesy of Delaware State Archives

NAME:	<u>JOHN R. WILLIAMS</u>
RIG:	Steam Screw
REGISTERED NUMBER:	211696
DATE & LOCATION BUILT:	1913; Port Richmond; New York for towing service
DATE SUNK:	June 24, 1942
REPORTED POSITION WHERE SUNK:	38°45'00"N 74°55'00"W in 48' of water (near Cape Henlopen)
OWNER:	Great Lakes Dredge & Dock Company of New Jersey 17 Battery Place New York, New York
MASTER AT TIME OF SINKING:	(13 man crew)
PHOTOGRAPH &/OR DRAWING:	Mariners Museum Photograph PB 2252
CONSTRUCTION:	steel; 396 gross tons; 269 net tons; length 136.7'; breadth 27.6'; depth 14.7'; 200 h.p. engine

Courtesy of the Mariners Museum, Newport News, Virginia 23606

NAME: JOHN SHAY

RIG: Schooner

DATE SUNK: September 19, 1901

REPORTED POSITION WHERE SUNK: 1-7/8 miles north of Cape Henlopen Station

MASTER AT TIME OF SINKING: Captain Sprague and 6 crew (all 7 persons saved)

HOME PORT: Sommers Point, New Jersey

LAST PORT SAILED FROM: New York

PORT BOUND FOR: Philadelphia, Pennsylvania

CONSTRUCTION: 305 tons

NAME:	JOHN W. HALL
RIG:	Schooner
REGISTERED NUMBER:	76920; Signal Letters KHWC
DATE & LOCATION BUILT:	1890 in Frederica, Delaware
DATE SUNK:	March 12, 1912 at 10:12 p.m.
REPORTED POSITION WHERE SUNK:	Ocean City, Maryland; stranded 3 miles south of station on outer bar 300 yards off beach
OWNER:	John W. Hall & Son (Hall & Lester); Mrs. Sarah E. Hall, Frederica, Delaware
MASTER AT TIME OF SINKING:	Captain W. H. Bennett of 32 South Street, New York, New York and 6 crewmen (all 7 saved)
CARGO AT TIME OF SINKING:	lumber (nearly all cargo saved)
HOME PORT:	Frederica, Delaware (Mrs. Sarah E. Hall, managing owner)
LAST PORT SAILED FROM:	Wilmington, North Carolina
PORT BOUND FOR:	New York
WEATHER CONDITIONS AT TIME OF SINKING:	fog, stormy, windy; 43°F.; flood tide; high seas
CONSTRUCTION:	wood; 3 masts; 346 gross tons; 329 net tons; single deck; length 131'; breadth 34'; depth 9'; materials - oak, yellow pine, galvanized iron fastenings
OTHER DATA:	wreck was sighted by Archie Cropper of Ocean City

NAME: JONESPORT

RIG: Barge (unrigged)

REGISTERED NUMBER: American 218181

DATE & LOCATION BUILT: 1919; Machias, Maine

DATE SUNK: February 18, 1937; 6:30 p.m.

REPORTED POSITION WHERE SUNK: off Ocean City, Maryland
38°17'33"N
75°00'00"W

OWNER: W. S. Stapp; Southern Transportation Company of New Jersey, Commercial Trust Building, Philadelphia, Pennsylvania

MASTER AT TIME OF SINKING: Captain S. Anderson
Post Office Box 66
Arlington, Jacksonville, Florida;
carried 1 man crew

CARGO AT TIME OF SINKING: coal (1,995 tons)

HOME PORT: Philadelphia, Pennsylvania

LAST PORT SAILED FROM: Norfolk, Virginia

PORT BOUND FOR: Allyne Pointe, Connecticut

WEATHER CONDITIONS AT TIME OF SINKING: gale force winds

CONSTRUCTION: wood; 1,322 gross tons; 1,174 net tons; length 230.6'; breadth 37.6'; depth 19.6'

OTHER DATA: U.S.C.G. stood by while attempts were made to tow barge to harbor.

NAME:	JOSEPH E. HOOPER (ex NORTHERN 41)
RIG:	Schooner-barge (formerly had 3 masts)
REGISTERED NUMBER:	221160 (Hull No. 388); Call Letters KNSY
DATE & LOCATION BUILT:	May 1921 at Cumberland Shipbuilders in South Portland, Maine
DATE SUNK:	foundered while in tow November 15, 1945
REPORTED POSITION WHERE SUNK:	1-1/2 miles south by east of Fenwick Island Lat. 74°58'42"N; Long. 38°27'50"W; verified by Loran C and onsite bearings to shore objects
OWNER:	Eastern Transportation Company, Baltimore, Maryland
MASTER AT TIME OF SINKING:	Captain Hooper (died in 1948) survived by 3 sons
CARGO AT TIME OF SINKING:	coal
HOME PORT:	Wilmington, Delaware
LAST PORT SAILED FROM:	Norfolk, Virginia
PORT BOUND FOR:	New York
WEATHER CONDITIONS AT TIME OF SINKING:	storm
PHOTOGRAPH &/OR DRAWING:	drawing of type 1944 ferris hull
CONSTRUCTION:	wood; length 267.3'; beam 46'; depth 23.6'; single deck; 6 hatches - 22' x 14', 4 watertight holds; 2,233 tons; yellow pine; fir; galvanized iron fastenings

OTHER DATA: June, 1974; completely broken up and spread out; remains extend up from bottom about 6'; iron fastenings are covered with large formations of Atlantic coral; some of wood hull is left; visability usually about 6' to 10'; wreck sits on a sand bottom in 40' of water.

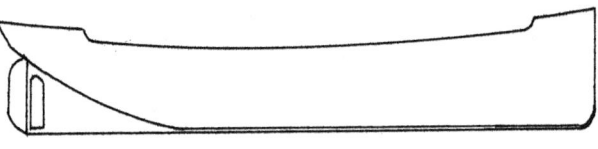

NAME: JUANITA

RIG: Barge

DATE SUNK: February 17, 1902

OWNER: M. A. McClary & T. McClary

CONSTRUCTION: iron hull; 1,165 tons; length 217'11"; beam 33'6"; depth 25'3"; engine 62"0 x 44" stroke (removed in 1893)

OTHER DATA: Vessel was being towed by the tug "MARS" which also lost the barge WESTERN BELLE at the same time.

NOTE: MVUS lists an iron hulled "Juanita" No. 13425, 1,244 gross tons; 1,218 net tons; length 206.5'; breadth 34.8'; depth 16.6'; built 1860 in Boston

NAME: JUNIPER

DATE SUNK: 1861

REPORTED POSITION WHERE SUNK: Winter Quarter Shoals

OTHER DATA: foundered

NAME: JUNO

RIG: Warship (Spanish)

DATE SUNK: October 29, 1802

REPORTED POSITION WHERE SUNK: Cape Henlopen

MASTER AT TIME OF SINKING: (425 persons lost)

CARGO AT TIME OF SINKING: 300,000 silver pesos

LAST PORT SAILED FROM: Mexico City

PORT BOUND FOR: Spain

CONSTRUCTION: 34 guns

NAME: KITTY

RIG: Schooner (snow)

REGISTERED NUMBER: British Registry

DATE SUNK: May 22, 1764

REPORTED POSITION WHERE SUNK: ashore on Assateague Island
                                 (burned to water line)

MASTER AT TIME OF SINKING: Captain Layton Albro; Mate
                                 William Ivory; Supercargo
                                 Edward Scott; Crew John Butler,
                                 Boynton Miller, John Keelar;
                                 2 sailors

CARGO AT TIME OF SINKING: (cargo lost) weapons; cotton;
                                 indigo

HOME PORT: Perthshire, England

LAST PORT SAILED FROM: New Providence, Bahama Island

PORT BOUND FOR: Philadelphia, Pennsylvania

NAME: LACEDEMONIENNE

RIG: Brig

DATE SUNK: January 1, 1799

REPORTED POSITION WHERE SUNK: Winter Quarter Shoals

NAME: LACEDAEMONIAN

DATE SUNK: July 12, 1798

REPORTED POSITION WHERE SUNK: Off Fenwick Shoals

OTHER DATA: Sunk by naval action. Part of
                                 ship's transom and name board came
                                 ashore on July 15.

NAME: LENAPE

RIG: Steam Screw (passenger service)

REGISTERED NUMBER: 210769 (Signal Letters LCRB)

DATE & LOCATION BUILT: 1912; Newport News, Virginia

DATE SUNK: November 18, 1925 (3:20 a.m.)

REPORTED POSITION WHERE SUNK: Delaware Breakwater north about 2 miles; beached 1/4 mile west end of the old breakwater; at high tide she floated free and started to drift towards the bay

EXACT POSITION: grounded in 18' of water at Lat. 38°49'25"N Long. 75°10'30" being towed there by Coast Guard boat no. 108

OWNER: American Clyde Lines, Pier 36, New York City

MASTER AT TIME OF SINKING: Captain Charles W. Devreux; 107 crewmen; 253 passengers; (1 person lost - Robert Leverton)

CARGO AT TIME OF SINKING: general

HOME PORT: New York City

LAST PORT SAILED FROM: New York City

PORT BOUND FOR: Jacksonville, Florida

WEATHER CONDITIONS
AT TIME OF SINKING: west/northwest wind at 5 knots; ebb tide; sea calm

PHOTOGRAPH &/OR DRAWING: Photograph No. 4504, courtesy of Steamship Historical Society

CONSTRUCTION: steel; 5,179 gross tons;, 3,889 net tons; wireless equipped; length 376.7'; breadth 50.1'; depth 20.6'; 3,500 h.p engine

OTHER DATA: burned; C.G.C. Kickapoo and Cold Spring Lifeboat rendered assistance. Classed by American Bureau of Shipping.

LENAPE

Courtesy of the Steamship Historical Society Collection,
University of Baltimore Library

NAME:	LEIV ERICKSON
RIG:	Schooner
REGISTERED NUMBER:	201891
DATE & LOCATION BUILT:	1905
DATE SUNK:	September 1, 1910 about 3:30 a.m.
REPORTED POSITION WHERE SUNK:	near Fenwick Island Shoals, Maryland about 1 mile off beach
OWNER:	Anton Christensen
MASTER AT TIME OF SINKING:	Anton Christensen, 615 Marcy Avenue, Brooklyn, New York; (15 persons aboard); 4 lost including Captain and Antonio Henrique, Frygve Martin, and a boy named Pete
CARGO AT TIME OF SINKING:	bluefish
HOME PORT:	New York
LAST PORT SAILED FROM:	Brooklyn, New York
PORT BOUND FOR:	fishing along coast
WEATHER CONDITIONS AT TIME OF SINKING:	light wind; smooth seas
CONSTRUCTION:	48 tons gross; 26 tons net
OTHER DATA:	While the LEIV ERICKSON was at anchor, the steamer CHESAPEAKE of 1,101 tons collided with her (according to Life Saving Service Casualty report).

NAME: **LEWIS CLARK**

RIG: Steamer

DATE SUNK: September 6, 1888

REPORTED POSITION WHERE SUNK: Point of Cape Henlopen

MASTER AT TIME OF SINKING: Captain Bartlett

HOME PORT: Bangor, Maine

CONSTRUCTION: 209 tons

NAME: **LIZZIE CRAWFORD**

RIG: Steam Tug

REGISTERED NUMBER: 140550

DATE & LOCATION BUILT: 1882; Camden, New Jersey

DATE SUNK: March 14, 1888

REPORTED POSITION WHERE SUNK: near beach at steamboat pier - Delaware Breakwater

MASTER AT TIME OF SINKING: Captain Kane

HOME PORT: Philadelphia, Pennsylvania

WEATHER CONDITIONS AT TIME OF SINKING: rain; storm

CONSTRUCTION: wood; 52.76 gross tons; 26.38 net tons; length 67.4'; breadth 17.5'; depth 8'; 130 h.p. engine

OTHER DATA: New York Times Thursday, March 15, 1888

NAME: LIZZIE THOMPSON

RIG: Schooner

DATE SUNK: 2:30 p.m.; Monday, April 16, 1883

REPORTED POSITION WHERE SUNK: 10 miles southeast of Cape May Lightship collision with steamship Nacoochee

MASTER AT TIME OF SINKING: 16 persons aboard Captain L. McKowan

CARGO AT TIME OF SINKING: 250 barrels of mackerel

HOME PORT: Newburyport, Massachusetts

LAST PORT SAILED FROM: Portland, Maine

PORT BOUND FOR: fishing cruise

WEATHER CONDITIONS AT TIME OF SINKING: fog

OTHER DATA: New York Times
A Schooner Lost at Sea

The Lizzie Thompson sunk in a collision with the Steam-ship Nacoochee The steam-ship Nacoochee, of the Savannah Line, which arrived here yesterday, was in collision with the schooner Lizzie Thompson last Monday, and the latter vessel went down a few moments afterward, but her crew of 18 men was rescued and brought to this port. Captain Kempton, of the steam- ship, reported that at 2:30 Monday afternoon, when about 10 miles south-east of the Cape May light-ship, the weather was thick and he was proceeding cautiously at the rate of six miles an hour. The lookout heard a voice in the fog right ahead, and the cry was repeated several times. Capt. Kempton ordered the engines to be reversed and the helm put to port. A schooner was then discovered close at hand on the starboard bow. Capt. Kempton, who was standing at the bow, called out to the master of the schooner to put his helm to port. The speed of the Nacoochee had been greatly reduced, but she was now too close to the Schooner to avoid a collision. The latter was struck on her port side just aft of the main rigging. A hole about a foot deep was made in her planking and extended below the watermark. The schooner began to fill rapidly. Her crew saw that it would be useless to attempt to save her. Three small boats were put over the side and the men took refuge in these, saving only what clothing they had on at the time. Capt. L. McKewen of the lost vessel, stated that he sailed from Portland on a fishing cruise about five weeks since. About 250 barrels of mackerel had been secured, and the schooner was returning home when the whistles of the Nacoochee were heard. The schooner's foghorn was blown, but it was not heard on board the steam ship. The vessel sailed from Newburyport, Mass., and was insured.

Copyright 1879/1880/1881/1883/1884/1887/1889/1895/1913/1918.
by The New York Times Company. Reprinted by permission.

NAME: **L.S. LEVERING**

RIG: Schooner

REGISTERED NUMBER: 15290; Signal Letters JBMG

DATE & LOCATION BUILT: 1876; Wilmington, Delaware

DATE SUNK: February 23, 1901

REPORTED POSITION WHERE SUNK: at point of Cape Henlopen

MASTER AT TIME OF SINKING: Captain Falkenberg and 5 crew (all 6 persons saved)

CARGO AT TIME OF SINKING: wood

HOME PORT: Sommers Point, New Jersey

LAST PORT SAILED FROM: Pamunkey River, Virginia

PORT BOUND FOR: New York, New York

CONSTRUCTION: 298.50 tons gross; 283.68 tons net; length 119.5'; breadth 29.5'; depth 9.4'

NAME: **LUCY E. FRIEND**

RIG: Schooner

REGISTERED NUMBER: 140553

DATE & LOCATION BUILT: July, 1882 by George E. Currier, Newburyport, Massachusetts

DATE SUNK: November 14, 1910

REPORTED POSITION WHERE SUNK: Fenwick Island

OWNER: W. H. Collins in 1910

MASTER AT TIME OF SINKING: crew of 7 (no one was lost)

HOME PORT: Gloucester, Massachusetts

CONSTRUCTION: wood; 3 masts; centerboard; 470 gross tons; 347 net tons; length 147'; breadth 34.6'; depth 12.6'; white oak, yellow pine, iron and copper fastenings

OTHER DATA: foundered

NAME:	LUCY NEFF (formerly W.P. Ketcham) named LUCY NEFF in 1902
RIG:	Steam screw
REGISTERED NUMBER:	American; 81441
DATE & LOCATION BUILT:	1893; West Bay City, Michigan; James Davidson, builder
DATE SUNK:	December 15, 1915 at 9 a.m.
REPORTED POSITION WHERE SUNK:	20 miles east of Fenwick Island
OWNER:	H. W. Cook of Michigan City, Indiana; then C. S. Neff of Milwaukee, Wisconsin; then Coast Steamship Company of Delaware
MASTER AT TIME OF SINKING:	Captain W. Laugharne of New York and 18 crewmen
CARGO AT TIME OF SINKING:	Dyewood (1,000 tons)
HOME PORT:	Wilmington, Delaware
LAST PORT SAILED FROM:	Jamaica
PORT BOUND FOR:	New York
WEATHER CONDITIONS AT TIME OF SINKING:	heavy seas
PHOTOGRAPH &/OR DRAWING:	Steamship Historical Society Photograph No. 1433
CONSTRUCTION:	wood; 946 gross tons; 759 net tons; length 225.0'; breadth 37.0'; depth 13.5'; oak; iron fastenings; engine = triple expansion steam 16", 25" and 42" diameter by 30" stroke built by Dry Dock Engine Works in Detroit with one cylindrical return tubular boiler 12'3" dia.x 11'7-1/2" long
OTHER DATA:	vessel foundered due to continuous strain

                                    S.S. CHASEHILL (British) took
                                    crew off in boats (all saved)
                                    vessel insured for about $15,000

The following was copied from newspaper article (exact wording):
                    <u>Philadelphia Public Ledger</u>
                    Friday Morning, December 17, 1915
                        Page 3, 5th Column

                    "SHIP SINKS OFF DELAWARE

New York, Dec. 16.
Crew is rescued ten minutes before the LUCY NEFF went down. Captain
Loughrane and the crew of 18 of the American steamer LUCY NEFF, which
foundered yesterday off the Delaware coast, arrived here today on the
British steamer Chasehill. Captain Loughrane said he sailed from
Falmouth, Jamaica, December 6 with a cargo of logwood intended for
American dye makers. After encountering high seas for several days the
LUCY NEFF sprung several leaks on the night of December 14. Ten minutes
after the last man had left the LUCY NEFF, she sank.

LUCY NEFF

Courtesy of the Steamship Historical Society Collection,
University of Baltimore Library

NAME: <u>LUTHER A. ROBY</u>

RIG: Schooner
REGISTERED NUMBER: 140721; K.C.Q.T.
DATE & LOCATION BUILT: 1884; Boston, Massachusetts
DATE SUNK: October 11, 1896
REPORTED POSITION WHERE SUNK: stranded at Cape Henlopen
MASTER AT TIME OF SINKING: 8 aboard; 3 lost
CARGO AT TIME OF SINKING: plaster
HOME PORT: Greenport, New York
LAST PORT SAILED FROM: Cheverie, N.S.
PORT BOUND FOR: Philadelphia, Pennsylvania
CONSTRUCTION: 639.51 tons gross; 607.53 tons net; length 158.2'; breadth 35.5'; depth 15.0'

NAME: <u>H.M.S. MAGDALEN</u>

REGISTERED NUMBER: (British)
DATE SUNK: 1780
REPORTED POSITION WHERE SUNK: Paramore Beach
OTHER DATA: driven ashore by the French

NAME: <u>MAID OF THE MIST</u>

RIG: Gas Screw
DATE & LOCATION BUILT: 1866
DATE SUNK: September 24, 1920
REPORTED POSITION WHERE SUNK: grounded off Cape Henlopen

NAME: <u>MAJOR WILLIAM H. TANTUM</u>

RIG: Schooner

REGISTERED NUMBER: 902522

DATE & LOCATION BUILT: 1873; Chester, Pennsylvania

DATE SUNK: September 10, 1889

REPORTED POSITION WHERE SUNK: 900' to the east of Lewes Station, 200 yards off beach

MASTER AT TIME OF SINKING: Captain Burns and 4 persons (all 5 saved by Lewes Station using Lyle gun and beach apparatus)

CARGO AT TIME OF SINKING: pig iron

HOME PORT: Philadelphia, Pennsylvania

LAST PORT SAILED FROM: Richmond, Virginia

PORT BOUND FOR: Middletown, Connecticut

WEATHER CONDITIONS
AT TIME OF SINKING: rough seas

CONSTRUCTION: 183.93 tons gross; 174.73 tons net; length 113.0'; breadth 23.4'; depth 8.2'

OTHER DATA: total loss

NAME: MANHATTAN

RIG: Steam Screw

REGISTERED NUMBER: 91194

DATE & LOCATION BUILT: 1879; John Roach's shipyard;
                                  Chester, Pennsylvania;
                                  launched Thursday, August 30, 1879

DATE SUNK: November 20, 1889 at 5:00 a.m.
                                  (collision)

REPORTED POSITION WHERE SUNK: near Fenwick Island about 8
                                  miles northeast of Fenwick Island
                                  Lightship in 16 fathoms (96')

EXACT POSITION: N 38° 27'23"
                                  W 74° 47'08"

OWNER: Old Dominion Steamship Company

MASTER AT TIME OF SINKING: Captain N. H. Jenny; Peter
                                  Nelson; QM - Liewellan Perkins;
                                  (14 saved, 11 lost - see
                                  attached report)

CARGO AT TIME OF SINKING: 200 tons of general merchandise

HOME PORT: New York

LAST PORT SAILED FROM: Beach Street, New York City

PORT BOUND FOR: West Point, Virginia

WEATHER CONDITIONS
AT TIME OF SINKING: clear

PHOTOGRAPH &/OR DRAWING: drawing on page 3464 "Scientific
                                  American Supplement" No. 218,
                                  March 6, 1880

CONSTRUCTION: 1,525 tons; iron; length 228.0';
                                  breadth 35.28'; depth 20.1';
                                  compound 2 cylinder engine;
                                  4 lifeboats; 2 boilers

OTHER DATA: collision with schooner Agnes
                                  Manning; she struck the
                                  MANHATTAN on her port bow just
                                  aft of the collision bulkhead;
                                  her mainmast stuck out of water
                                  3'; name was removed by divers
                                  from stern July 18, 1981 .

New York Times
Saturday, November 23, 1889

"Run Down By A Schooner" - The steamer MANHATTAN goes to the bottom - 11 lives probably lost - collision on a clear night, one of the boats capsizes. The iron steamship MANHATTAN of the Old Dominion Steamship Company was sunk on Wednesday morning at 5:00 a.m. about 8 miles northeast of Fenwick Island Lightship by the coal schooner Agnes Manning - MANHATTAN sank in 15 minutes, schooner ran on to Philadelphia.

MANHATTAN - built 1879 at John Roach's shipyard Chester, Pennsylvania; 225' L; 35' beam; 20' depth of hold; cargo 200 tons of general merchandise; settled by the head; lies in 16 fathoms; 4 lifeboats; MANHATTAN was heading south; mainmast stuck out of water 3'; Captain N. H. Jenny; Agnes Manning built Bath, Maine; 4 masts; MANHATTAN left Beach Street bound for West Point, Virginia; Officers - Peter Nelson; QM - Liewellan Perkins; schooner struck her port bow just aft of collision bulkhead; about 30' from stern; impact crashed all forerigging onto deck of MANHATTAN; 14 saved, 11 lost - 1 off of Agnes Manning)

Copyright 1879/1880/1881/1883/1884/1887/1889/1895/1913/1918 by The New York Times Company. Reprinted by permission.

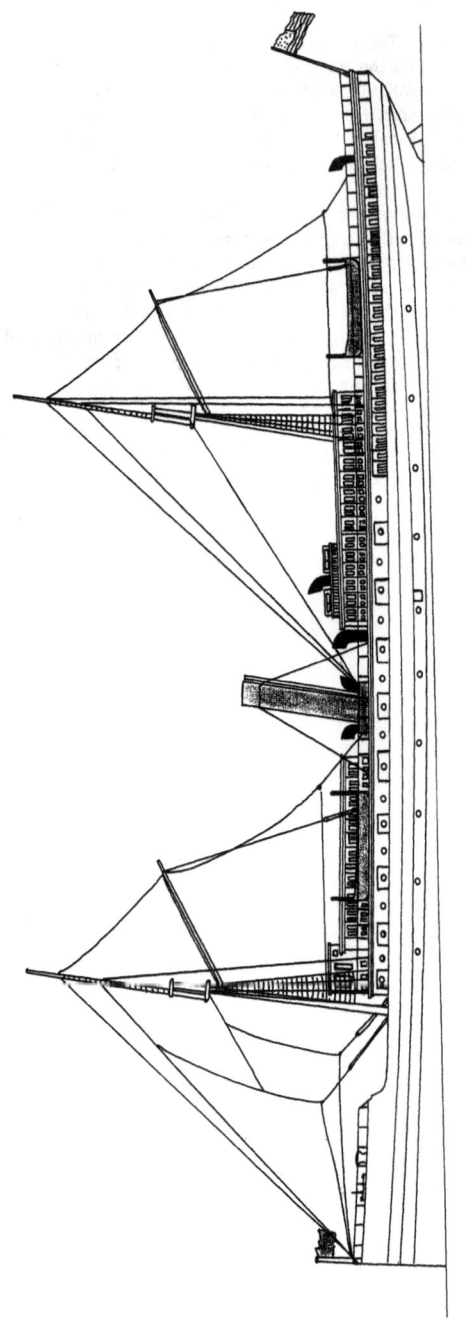

MANHATTAN

NAME: MARATHON

RIG: Brig

REGISTERED NUMBER: (American)

DATE SUNK: October 3, 1795

REPORTED POSITION WHERE SUNK: Gull Shoals

NAME: MARIA JOHANNA

DATE SUNK: March 10, 1784 at night

REPORTED POSITION WHERE SUNK: inside tip of Cape Henlopen on shore

MASTER AT TIME OF SINKING: Captain Pieter Yallings Bonk; 19 person lost; 21 persons on board; the supercargo and his clerk were saved by coming ashore on a plank

HOME PORT: Amsterdam

LAST PORT SAILED FROM: Amsterdam

PORT BOUND FOR: Philadelphia, Pennsylvania

WEATHER CONDITIONS AT TIME OF SINKING: gale

OTHER DATA: Maryland Gazette
April 1, 1784
(ship went to pieces)

NAME: MARIE C. BEAZLEY

RIG: Schooner Barge

DATE & LOCATION BUILT: 1918

DATE SUNK: reported as February 8, 1920;
                                    actually February 8, 1927

REPORTED POSITION WHERE SUNK: 10 miles north of Fenwick
                                    Island Lightship;
                                    38°33'N; 74°42'06"W

OWNER: Hedger Transportation Company

CARGO AT TIME OF SINKING: coal

LAST PORT SAILED FROM: Norfolk, Virginia

PORT BOUND FOR: Boston, Massachusetts

CONSTRUCTION: wood; 2,414 tons

OTHER DATA: vessel burned; U.S.C.G.C. Seminole
                                    attended wreck on February 9,
                                    1927; found wreck with mainmast
                                    and 2 booms above water; destroyed
                                    by mines; at the time of the
                                    accident, 5 coast guard cutters
                                    went to the rescue including the
                                    cutter Corwin

<u>New York Times</u>
February 9, 1927

BARGE AFIRE AT SEA: CREW REPORTED SAFE
As Coast Guard Speeds to Their Aid, Message Tells of Taking Off Men

Cape May, N.J. Feb. 9 - Five Coast Guard cutters early this morning were speeding to the assistance of the barge MARIE BEASLEY, which was reported by radio to be on fire ten miles north of the Fenwick Island Lightship, fifty miles from this place.

The first S.O.S. was picked up by the Coast Guard radio operator at Coast Guard Base 5 here at 11:25 last night. The distress signals were sent from the steamship Ballenas, which reported that she was standing by the burning barge. The five Coast Guard cutters, all seventy-five foot boats, were notified by radio to hurry to the assistance of the burning barge.

The nearest cutter was the C. G. Corwin, which reported that it was about twenty-three miles from the position of the barge.

According to word received here early this morning by the marine division of the Radio Corporation of America, men aboard the burning barge had been taken off and the barge abandoned. It is owned by the Hedger Transportation Company.

Copyright 1920/1927/* by The New York Times Company
Reprinted by permission.

NAME: <u>MARIE F. CUMMINS</u>

RIG: Schooner

REGISTERED NUMBER: 135823; Call Letters K.C.T.Q.

DATE & LOCATION BUILT: 1884; Mauricetown, New Jersey

DATE SUNK: November 14, 1908 about 9:00 p.m.

REPORTED POSITION WHERE SUNK: 2 miles north of Indian River Inlet, 1 mile north of station, 200 yards from beach

OWNER: Holt & Cummings

MASTER AT TIME OF SINKING: Capt. John N. Adam of Camden, New Jersey and 6 crewmen: H.H. Lallenentsen, Charles Brandford, Fred Miller, Martin Christianson, Nils Lufverson, Joseph Martin

CARGO AT TIME OF SINKING: empty oil barrels

HOME PORT: Philadelphia, Pennsylvania

LAST PORT SAILED FROM: Boston, Massachusetts

PORT BOUND FOR: Delaware Breakwater

WEATHER CONDITIONS AT TIME OF SINKING: stormy, light gale, easterly wind, rain, high surf

CONSTRUCTION: wood; 548 gross tons; 489 net tons; 3 masts; length 187.7'; breadth 34.9'; depth 15.0'

OTHER DATA: stranded - a wrecking crew attempted to refloat her on the 16th but abandoned her

NAME:	MARION CHAPPELL
RIG:	Schooner - barge
REGISTERED NUMBER:	93001
DATE & LOCATION BUILT:	December 20, 1899, Robert Palmer and Son Shipbuilding & Marine Railway Company, Noank, Connecticut
DATE SUNK:	October 10, 1925 at 8:00 p.m.
REPORTED POSITION WHERE SUNK:	six miles north of Fenwick Island Light, Maryland
OWNER:	Thomas Towboat Company, New London, Connecticut
MASTER AT TIME OF SINKING:	Capt. Morrill Law of Providence, Rhode Island and 3 crewmen
CARGO AT TIME OF SINKING:	Bituminous coal; 2,585 tons;
HOME PORT:	New London, Connecticut
LAST PORT SAILED FROM:	Norfolk, Virginia
PORT BOUND FOR:	Boston, Massachusetts
WEATHER CONDITIONS AT TIME OF SINKING:	70 m.p.h. wind; cloudy; heavy seas
CONSTRUCTION:	wood; 3 masts; 1,595 tons gross; 1,484 tons net; length 243.3'; breadth 43.8'; depth 22.0'
OTHER DATA:	being towed by the tug "Chappell" she foundered

NAME:	MARION O'BOYLE
RIG:	Barge
REGISTERED NUMBER:	168531
DATE & LOCATION BUILT:	1918; Stratford, Connecticut
DATE SUNK:	November 12, 1923
REPORTED POSITION WHERE SUNK:	near Fenwick Island Gas Bouy (off Fenwick Island Shoal)
OWNER:	Anthony O'Boyle 15 Moore Street New York, New York
MASTER AT TIME OF SINKING:	Capt. James Mathews, Shadyside, Maryland; Mrs. Mathews (wife) and daughter, total of 5 persons aboard; 2 seamen rescued. The Captain, his wife and daughter were drowned while trying to land lifeboat in surf near Short Ledge Light. However, according to a news article, they swam ashore safely.
CARGO AT TIME OF SINKING:	Bituminous coal
HOME PORT:	New York, New York
LAST PORT SAILED FROM:	Norfolk, Virginia
PORT BOUND FOR:	Boston, Massachusetts
WEATHER CONDITIONS AT TIME OF SINKING:	heavy seas and high winds
CONSTRUCTION:	wood; 2,200 gross tons
OTHER DATA:	The Marion O'Boyle foundered while in tow of the tug "Underwriter" about midnight.

MARION O'BOYLE
Report of Casualty

Tug anchored barges around 10:00 a.m. Nov. 12th around Fenwick Island Gas Buoy, barge was washing very badly and crew was forced to leave all anchor chains out to keep her from dragging ashore, barge started to leak and continued to get worse and Capt. was afraid that they could not hold her till morning as she was then gaining on the pumps. He then decided to get in the life boat along with the rest of the crew and headed for the shore in the darkness. All went well until the boat got in the breakers and overturned, two seamen were saved, but the captain, his wife and child were drowned.

NAME: H.M.S. MARLBOROUGH

DATE SUNK: November 29, 1762
REPORTED POSITION WHERE SUNK: 10 leagues off Maryland coast
CONSTRUCTION: 96 guns; 1,579 tons

NAME: MARQUIS de SEIGNELAY

DATE SUNK: August 22, 1788
REPORTED POSITION WHERE SUNK: off Maryland coast
CONSTRUCTION: 232 tons

NAME: MARY & LOUISE

RIG: Snow
DATE SUNK: September 17, 1739
REPORTED POSITION WHERE SUNK: Assateague Beach
OTHER DATA: aground

NAME: MARY ROGERS

RIG: Schooner
REGISTERED NUMBER: British
DATE SUNK: January 20, 1892
REPORTED POSITION WHERE SUNK: Delaware Breakwater
MASTER AT TIME OF SINKING: 6 persons aboard (1 lost)
CARGO AT TIME OF SINKING: asphalt
LAST PORT SAILED FROM: Trinidad
PORT BOUND FOR: Philadelphia
CONSTRUCTION: 138 tons

NAME: MASCOTTE

RIG: Bark
REGISTERED NUMBER: 92018; Call Letters K.F.G.P.
DATE & LOCATION BUILT: 1854; Roslyn, New York
DATE SUNK: February 12, 1888
REPORTED POSITION WHERE SUNK: Rehobeth Beach, Delaware
CONSTRUCTION: 24.07 gross tons; 22.87 net tons;
                                         length 51.8'; breadth 15.0';
                                         depth 4.4'

NAME:	<u>MATTIE W. ATWOOD</u>
RIG:	Schooner
REGISTERED NUMBER:	90439
DATE & LOCATION BUILT:	Essex, Massachusetts; 1872 by James & McKenzie
DATE SUNK:	December 18, 1887
REPORTED POSITION WHERE SUNK:	off Ocean City N38°20' W74°20'
OWNER:	Atwood & Rich
MASTER AT TIME OF SINKING:	T.E. Newcomb
HOME PORT:	Wellfleet
CONSTRUCTION:	oak; yellow pine; iron and copper fastenings; length 150'; breadth 33'; depth 17'; 653 tons; 2 decks; 3 masts

NAME:	<u>MERMAID</u>
REGISTERED NUMBER:	British
DATE SUNK:	1781

NAME:	<u>MERRIMAC</u>
RIG:	Schooner
REGISTERED NUMBER:	203197
DATE & LOCATION BUILT:	1906; Pocomoke City, Maryland
DATE SUNK:	April 10, 1918
REPORTED POSITION WHERE SUNK:	Rehobeth, Delaware
MASTER AT TIME OF SINKING:	3 man crew
HOME PORT:	Baltimore, Maryland
CONSTRUCTION:	640 gross tons; 595 net tons; length 182.6'; breadth 35.0'; depth 12.0'
OTHER DATA:	stranded

NAME:	MIMA A. REED
RIG:	Schooner
REGISTERED NUMBER:	90681; Signal Letters J.Q.H.K.
DATE & LOCATION BUILT:	November 1874 by Ramsdell & Rumball of Harrington, Maine; (Woodbury Leighton, Master Carpenter)
DATE SUNK:	September 10, 1889
REPORTED POSITION WHERE SUNK:	Delaware Breakwater, 1/4 mile N.N.E. of Lewes Station
OWNER:	O.P. Rumball
MASTER AT TIME OF SINKING:	Capt. Dixon; 8 persons aboard (all saved)
CARGO AT TIME OF SINKING:	coal
HOME PORT:	Machias, Maine
LAST PORT SAILED FROM:	Philadelphia, Pennsylvania
PORT BOUND FOR:	Boston, Massachusetts
CONSTRUCTION:	wood; 3 masts; 321 gross tons; 305.38 net tons; length 121.6'; breadth 31.3'; depth 11.8'; materials - various woods, iron and copper fastenings

NAME:	<u>MINNIE & GUSSIE</u>
RIG:	Schooner
REGISTERED NUMBER:	91531; Call Letters J.W.V.T.
DATE & LOCATION BUILT:	1882 in Tottenville, New York by J.S. Ellis
DATE SUNK:	January 30, 1891
REPORTED POSITION WHERE SUNK:	16 miles S.S.E. of Cape Henlopen
CONSTRUCTION:	227.56 tons gross; 216.19 tons net; length 114.4'; breadth 32.5'; depth 8.6'
OTHER DATA:	The U.S.C.G.C. Yantic, commander Rockwell ordered to cruise along the Atlantic Coast and destroy any wreck including the MINNIE & GUSSIE (New York times, February 11, 1891).

NAME:	<u>MONTGOMERY</u>
RIG:	Steam Screw
REGISTERED NUMBER:	16997
DATE & LOCATION BUILT:	1858; New York City
DATE SUNK:	January 7, 1877
REPORTED POSITION WHERE SUNK:	off Delaware Capes
MASTER AT TIME OF SINKING:	17 persons lost
HOME PORT:	New York City
CONSTRUCTION:	787 tons (1,100 tons in <u>Record</u>); 2 decks; length 198'; breadth 29'; depth 18'; 6' draft; white oak; iron and copper fastenings; yellow metaled; iron or steel "X" strapping over frames
OTHER DATA:	collision with Seminole

NAME: MOONSTONE (PY-9)

RIG: Yacht

REGISTERED NUMBER: U.S. Navy - Radio Call Letters N.B.M.P.

DATE & LOCATION BUILT: 1929 by Germania Werft in Kiel, Germany

DATE SUNK: October 15, 1943

REPORTED POSITION WHERE SUNK: 23.7 miles offshore Indian River Inlet
38°30'47"N
74°31'16"W

OWNER: acquired by U.S. Navy in February 10, 1941; commissioned April 10, 1941

HOME PORT: Charleston, South Carolina

LAST PORT SAILED FROM: Balboa

PORT BOUND FOR: Philadelphia, Pennsylvania

PHOTOGRAPH &/OR DRAWING: Mariners Museum Photo 121482

CONSTRUCTION: steel; 379 tons; length 171'9"; beam 26'9"; draft 10'6"

OTHER DATA: sits upright and intact in 126' of water; collision with "Greer" sank immediately with one life lost

MOONSTONE

Courtesy of the Mariners Museum, Newport News, Virginia 23606

NAME:	MORO CASTLE
RIG:	Bark
REGISTERED NUMBER:	17927; Call Letters H.G.B.S.
DATE & LOCATION BUILT:	1869; Mystic, Connecticut
DATE SUNK:	November 25, 1888, 9:00 a.m.
REPORTED POSITION WHERE SUNK:	bayside of the Delaware Breakwater
EXACT POSITION:	stone breakwater
MASTER AT TIME OF SINKING:	crew of 10 - all saved by walking across masts to the stone breakwater
CARGO AT TIME OF SINKING:	coal
HOME PORT:	Boston, Massachusetts
LAST PORT SAILED FROM:	Philadelphia, Pennsylvania
PORT BOUND FOR:	San Francisco, California
CONSTRUCTION:	3 masts; 404.36 gross tons; 384.14 net tons; length 127.0'; breadth 29.0'; depth 17.0'
OTHER DATA:	The MORO CASTLE parted her chains and drove into the stone breakwater. The Lewes Station gave shelter to crew for 2 days. Another MORO CASTLE much later grounded and burned off Ashbury Park, New Jersey.

NAME:	MOUNTAINEER
RIG:	Steam Packet
DATE & LOCATION BUILT:	1846
DATE SUNK:	June 26, 1850
REPORTED POSITION WHERE SUNK:	stranded on Cape Henlopen
CONSTRUCTION:	513 tons

NAME:	**NANCY JANE**
RIG:	Brig
DATE & LOCATION BUILT:	1835 in Newcastle, Maine
DATE SUNK:	January 16, 1846
REPORTED POSITION WHERE SUNK:	on beach at Berlin, Maryland (also reported as ashore on North Beach, Assateague); visible at low tide just north of the fence at State Park property
MASTER AT TIME OF SINKING:	Captain Godfrey
CARGO AT TIME OF SINKING:	general plus 50 half pipes of Brandy which washed ashore
HOME PORT:	registered in New York City in January 14, 1836
LAST PORT SAILED FROM:	New York
PORT BOUND FOR:	Richmond, Virginia
CONSTRUCTION:	133-71/95 tons; wood; length 79.2'; breadth 23'3"; depth 8'4-1/2"; single deck; square stern; billethead
OTHER DATA:	identification not completely verified; this ship had false registration records as she was a gun and liquor runner

NAME: NELFRED

RIG: Oil Screw (clamboat)

REGISTERED NUMBER: 218871

DATE & LOCATION BUILT: Elco Works at Bayonne, New Jersey

DATE SUNK: October 15, 1956

REPORTED POSITION WHERE SUNK: 12 miles off Cape May near Five Fathom Bank in 5 fathoms

OWNER: Sigvald Osmundsen

CONSTRUCTION: wood; length 78.0'; breadth 12.4'; depth 5.8'; 330 h.p. engine

OTHER DATA: Burned - Coast Guard attempted to save her but pumps could not keep her from going down by stern.

NAME: N. B. MORRIS

RIG: Bark

DATE SUNK: February 28, 1902

REPORTED POSITION WHERE SUNK: 1-1/4 miles north of Cape Henlopen Station

MASTER AT TIME OF SINKING: Captain Stuart and 9 persons (all 10 saved)

CARGO AT TIME OF SINKING: bones

HOME PORT: Parrsboro, Nova Scotia

LAST PORT SAILED FROM: Rosario, South America

PORT BOUND FOR: Philadelphia, Pennsylvania

CONSTRUCTION: 709 tons

NAME: NEOSHO

RIG: Schooner
DATE & LOCATION BUILT: 1888
DATE SUNK: August 18, 1919
REPORTED POSITION WHERE SUNK: Fenwick Light Vessel, Delaware
CONSTRUCTION: 1,857 tons
OTHER DATA: foundered

NAME: NETTIE R. WILLING

RIG: Schooner
REGISTERED NUMBER: 130238
DATE & LOCATION BUILT: 1882; Kennebunk, Maine
DATE SUNK: April, 1903
REPORTED POSITION WHERE SUNK: off coast of Delaware
MASTER AT TIME OF SINKING: 4 persons aboard (4 lost)
CARGO AT TIME OF SINKING: oysters
HOME PORT: New Berne, North Carolina
LAST PORT SAILED FROM: Hampton, Virginia
PORT BOUND FOR: Marsh River, Delaware
CONSTRUCTION: 55.61 tons gross; 52.83 net tons; length 65.2'; breadth 22.1'; depth 6.0'

NAME:	NEW ORLEANS
RIG:	Steam Screw Passenger Service
REGISTERED NUMBER:	18726
DATE & LOCATION BUILT:	1872; Wilmington, Delaware
DATE SUNK:	October 11, 1917 (10th)
REPORTED POSITION WHERE SUNK:	38°41'00" N 74°51'00" W
	(north of Indian River Inlet) 10 miles from Cape Henlopen Lighthouse
MASTER AT TIME OF SINKING:	27 crew (1 life lost)
CARGO AT TIME OF SINKING:	sulphur
HOME PORT:	Wilmington, Delaware
LAST PORT SAILED FROM:	Sabine, New York
PHOTOGRAPH &/OR DRAWING:	Steamship Society of America, Inc. Number 579
CONSTRUCTION:	iron; 1,564 gross tons; 1,107 net tons; length 249.0'; breadth 33.0'; depth 24.4'; 1,100 h.p. engine
OTHER DATA:	foundered

NEW ORLEANS

Courtesy of the Steamship Historical Society Collection,
University of Baltimore Library

NAME:	U.S.S. NINA
RIG:	Steam Screw
DATE & LOCATION BUILT:	May 27, 1865; Reaney, Son & Archbold; Chester, Pennsylvania
DATE SUNK:	February 6, 1910
REPORTED POSITION WHERE SUNK:	"Listed as missing somewhere between Norfolk and Boston."
	3 miles north of R-2 Horn buoy Old Loran: 52374 70354
OWNER:	United States Navy
MASTER AT TIME OF SINKING:	one officer and 30 crew - all lost
CARGO AT TIME OF SINKING:	none
HOME PORT:	submarine flotilla base; Newport, Rhode Island
LAST PORT SAILED FROM:	Norfolk, Virginia
PORT BOUND FOR:	Boston, Massachusetts
WEATHER CONDITIONS AT TIME OF SINKING:	full gale
PHOTOGRAPH &/OR DRAWING:	U.S. Navy Photo Number NH-62007
CONSTRUCTION:	steel - converted tug rig; wood deck, wood superstructure; 420 tons; length 137'; breadth 26'; draft 9'10"
OTHER DATA:	As of September 1977, wreck sits upright in 75' of water and is fairly intact; wreck extends off sand bottom about 6' to 9'. Propeller (8' diameter) is still mounted. Parts of wood deck have collapsed. Entire wreck has abundance of Atlantic Coral, sea whips and fish. Several articles have been retrieved, such as binnacle, skylight covers, valves, gauges (marked "U.S.N.") and two diving helmets. Name also has been removed.

Courtesy of the United States Navy

NAME:	NORENA
RIG:	Schooner (formerly rigged as a bark)
DATE & LOCATION BUILT:	1874; Bath, Maine
DATE SUNK:	September 10, 1889
REPORTED POSITION WHERE SUNK:	1/4 mile west of Lewes Station, 200 yards from shore
MASTER AT TIME OF SINKING:	Captain Chase and 7 persons; all 8 saved by "life-car" line to shore
CARGO AT TIME OF SINKING:	coal
HOME PORT:	Portland, Maine
LAST PORT SAILED FROM:	Philadelphia, Pennsylvania
PORT BOUND FOR:	Portland, Maine
WEATHER CONDITIONS AT TIME OF SINKING:	heavy rain; high winds; rough seas
CONSTRUCTION:	439 tons; length 129'4"; breadth 33'1"; depth 14'6"
OTHER DATA:	total loss at time of running ashore; the vessel parted her chains and drove up on the outer bar

NAME: **NORTHERN PACIFIC**

RIG: Passenger Steamscrew

REGISTERED NUMBER: 212926; Signal Letters LFDP

DATE & LOCATION BUILT: 1915 by William Cramp and Sons Ship and Engine Building Company of Philadelphia

DATE SUNK: February 8, 1922 (burned)

REPORTED POSITION WHERE SUNK: 40 miles due east of Cape May

OWNER: 1st Owner: Great Northern Pacific Steamship Company

At Time Of Sinking: Admiral Line, H. F. Alexander, President

MASTER AT TIME OF SINKING: Captain William Lusti and 27 crew men and 4 draftmen employees of Sun Shipyard (these 4 men were lost); Mr. A. B. Wilson was second officer

CARGO AT TIME OF SINKING: ballast

HOME PORT: Astoria, Oregon

LAST PORT SAILED FROM: Hoboken, New Jersey

PORT BOUND FOR: Chester, Pennsylvania

WEATHER CONDITIONS AT TIME OF SINKING: fair

PHOTOGRAPH &/OR DRAWING: Mariners Museum Photo PB 26841

CONSTRUCTION: triple screw; steel; 8,255 tons; length 509.5'; breadth 63.1'; depth 21'; propelled by 3 Parsons turbines; average speed 23 knots; 20,000 h.p. engine

OTHER DATA: The Steamer Transportation, C. G. Cutters Kickapoo and Gresham and tanker Herbert G. Wylie stood by; wreck is upside down in 145' of water; keel comes to within 110' of the surface

NORTHERN PACIFIC
Courtesy of the Mariners Museum, Newport News, Virginia 23606

NAME:	NORTHERN 35
RIG:	Schooner-Barge
REGISTERED NUMBER:	219829
DATE & LOCATION BUILT:	1920; Manistee, Michigan
DATE SUNK:	February 14, 1927
REPORTED POSITION WHERE SUNK:	off Five Fathom Bank in 102' of water 38°45' N 74°38' W
OWNER:	Northern Barge Corporation of Delaware, Equitable Building, Wilmington, Delaware
HOME PORT:	Wilmington, Delaware
LAST PORT SAILED FROM:	Hampton Roads, Virginia
PORT BOUND FOR:	Providence, Rhode Island
CONSTRUCTION:	wood; 3 masts; 2,051 gross tons; 1,907 net tons; length 246.2'; breadth 43.0'; depth 24.4'
OTHER DATA:	foundered; on February 14, 1927, the U.S.C.G.C. Seminole attended wreck exploding mines on her and leaving 87' over the wreck

NAME: NORUMBEGA

RIG: Schooner

REGISTERED NUMBER: 130477; Call Letters KHFL

DATE & LOCATION BUILT: 1890; Essex, Massachusetts

DATE SUNK: April 23, 1906

REPORTED POSITION WHERE SUNK: Fenwick Island, Maryland

MASTER AT TIME OF SINKING: 18 persons aboard; 1 lost

HOME PORT: Gloucester, Massachusetts

LAST PORT SAILED FROM: New York City

PORT BOUND FOR: fishing trip

CONSTRUCTION: 126 tons gross; 91 tons net; length 107.5'; breadth 24.0'; depth 10.5'

OTHER DATA: collision with Schooner Edith L. Allen

NAME: **NUMBER SIX**

RIG: Schooner - barge

REGISTERED NUMBER: 130782; Call Letters KNMP

DATE & LOCATION BUILT: 1898; Bath, Maine

DATE SUNK: April 3, 1915 at noon

REPORTED POSITION WHERE SUNK: stranded on Hen and Chicken Shoal, Delaware

MASTER AT TIME OF SINKING: 5 lives lost (all on board) including Captain Johnson of Baltimore

CARGO AT TIME OF SINKING: coal

HOME PORT: Baltimore, Maryland

LAST PORT SAILED FROM: Baltimore, Maryland

PORT BOUND FOR: Boston, Massachusetts

WEATHER CONDITIONS AT TIME OF SINKING: snowstorm and 60 mph winds

CONSTRUCTION: 915 tons gross; 793 tons net; length 192.3'; breadth 35.1' depth 17.0'

OTHER DATA: sank while in tow of tug "Cumberland"

NAME: NUMBER NINE

RIG: Schooner - barge

REGISTERED NUMBER: 130806; Call Letters KNVC

DATE & LOCATION BUILT: 1899; Bath, Maine

DATE SUNK: April 3, 1915 at noon

REPORTED POSITION WHERE SUNK: grounded on Hen and Chicken Shoal, Delaware

CARGO AT TIME OF SINKING: coal

HOME PORT: Baltimore, Maryland

LAST PORT SAILED FROM: Baltimore, Maryland

PORT BOUND FOR: Boston, Massachusetts

WEATHER CONDITIONS AT TIME OF SINKING: snowstorm and 60 mph winds

CONSTRUCTION: 909 tons gross; 794 tons net; length 192.8'; breadth 35.1' depth 17.0'

OTHER DATA: Sank while in tow of tug "Cumberland", according to New York Times April 4.

NAME: NUMBER ELEVEN

RIG: Schooner

REGISTERED NUMBER: 130810; Call Letters KNWP

DATE & LOCATION BUILT: 1899; Bath, Maine

DATE SUNK: February 28, 1906

REPORTED POSITION WHERE SUNK: 10 miles E.S.E. off
                                     Fenwick Island Lightship

MASTER AT TIME OF SINKING: 5 persons aboard (all 5 lost)

CARGO AT TIME OF SINKING: coal

HOME PORT: Baltimore, Maryland

LAST PORT SAILED FROM: Baltimore, Maryland

PORT BOUND FOR: Boston, Massachusetts

CONSTRUCTION: wood, 953 tons gross; 840 net
                                     tons; length 189.9';
                                     breadth 35.5'; depth 18.1'

OTHER DATA: Foundered while in tow.

NAME: <u>OAKDENE</u>

RIG: Steamship

DATE & LOCATION BUILT: 1884 at Sunderland, England

DATE SUNK: March 2, 1895

REPORTED POSITION WHERE SUNK: ashore at Assateague Beach

MASTER AT TIME OF SINKING: J. A. Sandall and 19 crew members - all rescued

LAST PORT SAILED FROM: Hamburg

PORT BOUND FOR: Baltimore via Halifax, N. S.

CONSTRUCTION: 240' long, 38' beam, 18' draft; 996 tons

OTHER DATA:

Monday, March 4, 1895
<u>New York Times</u>

LEWES - Del., March 3. - The British steamship OAKDENE, from Hamburg, via Halifax, for Baltimore, which went ashore yesterday at Assateague Beach, filled and sank last night, and will probably be a total loss.

Sixteen of the crew, including the officers, were taken off by the wrecking tug North America and brought here. The rest of the crew, four men, were landed by lifesavers.

The OAKDENE was built at Sunderland, England, in 1884, and was 240 feet long, 38 feet beam, and 18 feet draught. Her tonnage was 996. She was commanded by J. A. Sandall, and was owned by G. T. Lam & Co. of Sunderland.

Copyright 1879/1880/1881/1883/1884/1887/1889/1895/1913/1918 by The New York Times Company. Reprinted by permission.

NAME: O.C. CLEARY

RIG: Brig

DATE SUNK: Monday, November 12, 1883

REPORTED POSITION WHERE SUNK: 5 miles southwest of Cape May; collision with Schooner "Royal Arch"

MASTER AT TIME OF SINKING: Captain John McCumbe

CARGO AT TIME OF SINKING: 8,000 bushels of salt and $300 gold belonging to Captain

LAST PORT SAILED FROM: Turks Island

PORT BOUND FOR: New Haven, Connecticut

OTHER DATA:

November 17, 1883
<u>New York Times</u>

A Brig Run Down and Sunk

Philadelphia, Nov. 16 - the brig O.C. CLEARY, Capt. John McCumbe, from Turks Island for New Haven, Conn., with 8,000 bushels of salt, was run into on Monday at 6 A.M. by the schooner "Royal Arch" of Boston, off Cape May, bearing south-west five miles. The CLEARY was struck amidship and cut clear through to the main hatch, and sank in 10 minutes. The Captain and crew jumped aboard the "Royal Arch", saving only the clothes they stood in. The Captain also lost $300 in gold. When struck the CLEARY was heading north-east and sailing by the wind, and the "Royal Arch" was heading south-east and running before the wind.

Copyright 1879/1880/1881/1883/1884/1887/1889/1895/1913/1918 by The New York Times Company. Reprinted by permission.

NAME: OCEAN BIRD

REGISTERED NUMBER: (British)

DATE SUNK: January 2, 1799

REPORTED POSITION WHERE SUNK: on beach at present day
                                     Assateague Beach; wrecked
                                     at Sinepauxent Inlet

CARGO AT TIME OF SINKING: Immigrants

OTHER DATA: Foundered; reportedly this
                                     vessel has been uncovered
                                     recently on the beach.

NAME: OCEANUS

RIG: Schooner

REGISTERED NUMBER: 19214; Call Letters J.D.Q.K.

DATE & LOCATION BUILT: 1865; Stoneybrook, New York

REPORTED POSITION WHERE SUNK: Delaware Capes

DATE SUNK: September 28, 1890

HOME PORT: Port Jefferson, New York

CONSTRUCTION: 254.16 gross tons; 241.66 net
                                     tons; length 112.8';
                                     breadth 30.4'; depth 8.4'

NAME:	O. D. WITHERELL
RIG:	Schooner
REGISTERED NUMBER:	19400' Signal Letters J.P.B.H.
DATE & LOCATION BUILT:	1874; Bath, Maine
DATE SUNK:	April 21, 1911
REPORTED POSITION WHERE SUNK:	Fenwick Island Light, Delaware; 1-1/2 miles north of Life Saving Station
CARGO AT TIME OF SINKING:	ballast
HOME PORT:	Dennis, Massachusetts
LAST PORT SAILED FROM:	New York, New York
PORT BOUND FOR:	Philadelphia, Pennsylvania
CONSTRUCTION:	wood, 3 masts; 631 tons gross; 599 tons net; length 148.0'; breadth 33.1'; depth 15.1'
OTHER DATA:	stranded

NAME:	<u>OLIVE BRANCH</u>
RIG:	Brig
DATE & LOCATION BUILT:	1812
DATE SUNK:	September 10, 1846
REPORTED POSITION WHERE SUNK:	on outer bar at Lewes, Delaware
OWNER:	William Gray
MASTER AT TIME OF SINKING:	Captain Emerson and crew (all saved)
CARGO AT TIME OF SINKING:	coal
LAST PORT SAILED FROM:	Philadelphia, Pennsylvania
PORT BOUND FOR:	Boston, Massachusetts
CONSTRUCTION:	34-50/95th ton burthen
OTHER DATA:	The Maryland Gazette mentions a ship named OLIVE BRANCH in operation May 10, 1764 under Captain Robertson.

NAME: PASSIAC

RIG: Schooner - Barge

REGISTERED NUMBER: 150721; Call Letters KMSC

DATE & LOCATION BUILT: 1896; Noank, Connecticut

DATE SUNK: May 27, 1922

REPORTED POSITION WHERE SUNK: 12 miles south of Fenwick Island

CARGO AT TIME OF SINKING: coal

HOME PORT: New York

LAST PORT SAILED FROM: Norfolk, Virginia

PORT BOUND FOR: New York

CONSTRUCTION: wood; 3 masts; 876 tons gross; 791 tons net; length 192.0'; breadth 34.7'; depth 16.4'

NAME: PATRIOT

RIG: Bark

DATE SUNK: May 23, 1889

REPORTED POSITION WHERE SUNK: Delaware Breakwater

NAME: PATTIE MORRISETTE

RIG: Barge

REGISTERED NUMBER: 215821

DATE & LOCATION BUILT: 1917; Deibert Barge Building
                               Company; Havre de Grace,
                               Maryland

DATE SUNK: January 24, 1935

REPORTED POSITION WHERE SUNK: 38°37'18"N
                               74°43'00"W in 60' of water

CARGO AT TIME OF SINKING: coal

LAST PORT SAILED FROM: Norfolk, Virginia

PORT BOUND FOR: New York

CONSTRUCTION: wood; 971 tons; length 204';
                               breadth 35.0'; depth 14.6'

OTHER DATA: foundered while in tow of tug
                               "Peter J. Hopper" attended by
                               "C.G.C. Champlain"

January 25, 1935
New York Times

Three Lost From Barge

Swept Into Sea As Craft Breaks Loose From Tug Off Cape May

CAPE MAY, N.J., Jan. 24 - As Coast Guardsmen of the cutter "Champlain" neared them early today three members of the barge, PATTIE MORRISETTE, which had broken loose from its tug, the Peter J. Hopper, during the night, were swept to their deaths by the high seas thirty miles from here in the Atlantic Ocean.

The "Champlain" cruised in the vicinity for more than an hour in the hope of picking up the men, and then steamed off in an effort to locate the tug, which had been reported in distress by radio. The identity of the three men will not be known until the tug is found.

The steamer "Berwingier" saw the plight of the Hopper and her string of three barges and reported it by radio to the Coast Guard. The "Champlain", cruising along the New Jersey coast, picked up the message and reached the barge in time to see one man swept overboard.

NAME: **PATUXENT**

RIG: Schooner

DATE & LOCATION BUILT: 1833 in Somerset County, Maryland

DATE SUNK: December 19, 1846

REPORTED POSITION WHERE SUNK: Delaware Breakwater

MASTER AT TIME OF SINKING: Captain Underhill and crew all believed lost

CARGO AT TIME OF SINKING: coal

HOME PORT: Registered in New York October 7, 1843

LAST PORT SAILED FROM: Philadelphia, Pennsylvania

PORT BOUND FOR: New York

WEATHER CONDITIONS AT TIME OF SINKING: gale

CONSTRUCTION: 95 tons

NAME: **PHANTOM**

RIG: Steamer Yacht

REGISTERED NUMBER: 150737

DATE & LOCATION BUILT: 1896; Camden, New Jersey

DATE SUNK: April 9, 1904

REPORTED POSITION WHERE SUNK: 1 mile south of Indian River Inlet Station

MASTER AT TIME OF SINKING: Captain Adkins and 2 persons (all 3 saved)

HOME PORT: Philadelphia, Pennsylvania

LAST PORT SAILED FROM: Philadelphia, Pennsylvania

PORT BOUND FOR: Indian River Inlet

CONSTRUCTION: 10 tons gross; 7 tons net; length 34.3'; breadth 4.8'; depth 4.7'

NAME:	POSEIDON
RIG:	Steamship (screw)
DATE & LOCATION BUILT:	1914; U.S. Shipping Board, Dunlop, Bremer and Company
DATE SUNK:	Wednesday, July 31, 1918
REPORTED POSITION WHERE SUNK:	off Delaware Capes 5 miles N.N.E. of Five Fathom Bank Lightship
MASTER AT TIME OF SINKING:	37 persons aboard; 33 survived (captain lost)
CARGO AT TIME OF SINKING:	none
LAST PORT SAILED FROM:	Boston, Massachusetts
PORT BOUND FOR:	Norfolk, Virginia
CONSTRUCTION:	steel; 1,909 gross tons; 1,008 net tons; 295.8' x 43.2' x 17.2'; 217 nominal h.p. engine triple expansion
OTHER DATA:	According to New York Times article of August 2, 1918, she collided with the Standard Oil Tanker Somerset (9,773 tons).

NAME:	**POWHATTAN**
RIG:	Oil Screw (fishing vessel)
DATE & LOCATION BUILT:	1931; Hampton, Virginia
DATE SUNK:	April 10, 1961
REPORTED POSITION WHERE SUNK:	43 miles southeast of Cape May in 32 fathoms
OWNER:	James Sands Darling, Jr., Newport News, Virginia
MASTER AT TIME OF SINKING:	Captain Severn Robbins
CONSTRUCTION:	61 gross tons; 23 net; length 77.5'; breadth 19.6'; depth 6.6'; 210 h.p. engine
OTHER DATA:	Collided with South African Pioneer bound from Charleston to New York at 6:00 A.M.; 1 survivor picked up; fishing vessel cut in half

NAME:	**PORPOIS**
RIG:	Brigantine
DATE SUNK:	September 22, 1855
REPORTED POSITION WHERE SUNK:	North Beach at Assateague (ashore)

NAME:	**POSTILLON**
RIG:	Schooner
DATE SUNK:	February 2, 1803
REPORTED POSITION WHERE SUNK:	Great Gull Shoals
MASTER AT TIME OF SINKING:	(entire crew lost)
WEATHER CONDITIONS AT TIME OF SINKING:	blizzard
CONSTRUCTION:	110 tons

NAME: PRINCESS ANN

RIG: Ship

DATE & LOCATION BUILT   (British)

DATE SUNK: February 2, 1698

REPORTED POSITION WHERE SUNK: Assateague Beach

OTHER DATA: completely broke up

NAME: PRINCESS CAROLINE

RIG: Ship

DATE & LOCATION BUILT   (British)

DATE SUNK: April, 1903

REPORTED POSITION WHERE SUNK: aground on Winter Quarter
                                  Shoals

CONSTRUCTION: 350 tons

OTHER DATA: broke up; Maine Maritime Museum
                                  can find no record of this
                                  vessel.

NAME: PRINCIPESSA MARGHARTA
                                  de PIEMONTE

RIG: Bark

DATE SUNK: March 12, 1891

REPORTED POSITION WHERE SUNK: Hen and Chicken Shoal

NAME:	**P. TEE**
RIG:	Oil Screw
REGISTERED NUMBER:	269085
DATE SUNK:	May 27, 1970; 10:30 p.m.
REPORTED POSITION WHERE SUNK:	Hen and Chicken Shoal, 1/2 mile from Harbor of Refuge Light Station
	38°47'77"N 75° 5'00"W
OWNER:	Joseph Zanks Indian River Boat Association Box 800 Rehobeth, Delaware 19971
MASTER AT TIME OF SINKING:	Joseph Zanks
CARGO AT TIME OF SINKING:	none
HOME PORT:	Indian River, Delaware
LAST PORT SAILED FROM:	Indian River Boat Basin
PORT BOUND FOR:	Lewes, Delaware
WEATHER CONDITIONS AT TIME OF SINKING:	clear, 3 to 4 ft. seas; 10 knot wind
CONSTRUCTION:	converted PT boat; plywood hull; twin engines; length 72'; draft 5'; 61 gross tons
OTHER DATA:	The "P. TEE" was towing the dredge Nanticoke. In an unsafe maneuver, the dredge struck the stern of the P. TEE causing her to sink. The dredge eventually was worked onto shore and salvaged. Wreck was completely broken up; several pieces and bow section washed up on shore; engines and part of midsection are lying on sand bottom.

NAME: <u>PYLADES</u>

DATE SUNK: December 3, 1810

REPORTED POSITION WHERE SUNK: Assateague Beach

CARGO AT TIME OF SINKING: china and pottery

NAME: QUANGO

RIG: Brig

DATE SUNK: February 3, 1880

REPORTED POSITION WHERE SUNK: on the ice breaker -
                                 Delaware Breakwater and then
                                 drifted on Plum Point Shoal

CARGO AT TIME OF SINKING: sugar and molasses

HOME PORT: Prince Edward Island

LAST PORT SAILED FROM: Demerara

OTHER DATA: crew was taken off by tug
                                 "Pioneer"

February 4, 1880
New York Times

Tidings of Marine Loss

Wrecks Scattered Along The Coast From Maine to North Carolina

Gloucester, Mass., Feb. 3. - The fishing schooner "Winifred J. King" went ashore on the back side of Eastern Point this morning, in a thick snow-storm, and soon went to pieces. The crew was saved. The schooner was owned by John King, was valued at $4,353, and was insured for $4,470 in the Gloucester Mutual Fishing Insurance Company.

Marshfield, Mass., Feb. 3. - The three-masted schooner "Mary J. Castner", from New Orleans, loaded with cotton, is ashore in Marshfield Bridge, opposite Abington Village. She can possibly be saved as the damage is slight.

College Point, Long Island, Feb. 3. - The schooner "Emma Lewis Higbee", of Hoboken, bound for Huntington, with a cargo of coal, anchored in Cow Bay, and on Monday night, parted her chains and came ashore at Plumb Point.

Lewes, Del., Feb. 3. - The brig QUANGO, of Prince Edward Island, from Demerara, with sugar and molasses for Delaware Breakwater, ran on the end of the ice-breaker at 11 o'clock last night, during the storm. Beginning to sink, she was abandoned by her crew, who went aboard the schooner "Henry Parker", where they remained until this evening, when they were taken off by the tug "Pioneer" and landed here. The vessel drifted on Plum Point Shoal, where she now lies, full of water, with her masts and stern gone. Part of her cargo will probably be saved in a damaged condition, but the vessel will be a total loss.

Copyright 1879/1880/1881/1883/1884/1887/1889/1895/1913/1918
by The New York Times Company. Reprinted by permission.

NAME:	**QUATTRO**
RIG:	Bark
DATE & LOCATION BUILT:	1871; Sestri, Italy
DATE SUNK:	February 17, 1887
REPORTED POSITION WHERE SUNK:	Ocean City, Maryland 150 yards off beach opposite 79th Street in 17' of water
MASTER AT TIME OF SINKING:	1886; E. Avonzo
HOME PORT:	Genoa, Italy
CONSTRUCTION:	977 tons; 2 decks; 177.7' x 32.5' x 22.6'; oak, pine; iron and copper fastenings

NAME:	**RACEHORSE**
DATE SUNK:	November 15, 1777
REPORTED POSITION WHERE SUNK:	off Lewes, Delaware
CONSTRUCTION:	16 guns, 385 tons
OTHER DATA:	Burned by American forces to prevent capture.

NAME:	<u>RAPIDAN</u> (formerly Catharine C.)
RIG:	Steam Yacht
REGISTERED NUMBER:	126989; Signal Letters KQWC
DATE & LOCATION BUILT:	1893; Wyandotte, Michigan
DATE SUNK:	September 10, 1901
REPORTED POSITION WHERE SUNK:	2 miles north of Cape Henlopen Station
MASTER AT TIME OF SINKING:	Captain Staples and 11 persons (all 12 saved)
HOME PORT:	Chicago, Illinois
LAST PORT SAILED FROM:	New York City, New York
CONSTRUCTION:	82 tons; 58 net tons; length 106.6'; breadth 17.3'; depth 8.5'

NAME:	<u>RED WING</u>
RIG:	Schooner
REGISTERED NUMBER:	21567
DATE & LOCATION BUILT:	1860; Noank, Connecticut
DATE SUNK:	October 23, 1891
REPORTED POSITION WHERE SUNK:	Indian River Inlet
MASTER AT TIME OF SINKING:	6 aboard, 6 lost
CARGO AT TIME OF SINKING:	fishing trip
HOME PORT:	Noank, Connecticut
LAST PORT SAILED FROM:	New York City, New York
CONSTRUCTION:	28.23 tons gross; 26.82 tons net; length 50.5'; breadth 17.2'; depth 7.0'

NAME:	**RETURN**
RIG:	Sloop
DATE SUNK:	December 9, 1787
REPORTED POSITION WHERE SUNK:	near Cape Henlopen
MASTER AT TIME OF SINKING:	Captain Perine
LAST PORT SAILED FROM:	New Providence
PORT BOUND FOR:	New York
OTHER DATA:	"Maryland Gazette" Thursday, January 18, 1787

NAME:	**RETRIBUTION**
RIG:	Ship
DATE SUNK:	1839
REPORTED POSITION WHERE SUNK:	Assateague Beach
MASTER AT TIME OF SINKING:	all hands lost
CONSTRUCTION:	1,200 tons
OTHER DATA:	foundered

NAME:	**RIVERDALE**
RIG:	Schooner
DATE SUNK:	March 30, 1884
REPORTED POSITION WHERE SUNK:	Delaware Breakwater
CARGO AT TIME OF SINKING:	pinewood
LAST PORT SAILED FROM:	Lewes, Delaware
PORT BOUND FOR:	Philadelphia, Pennsylvania
CONSTRUCTION:	74 tons

NAME: R. F. LOPER

RIG: Brig

DATE SUNK: December 16, 1841

REPORTED POSITION WHERE SUNK: Sinapuxton Shoals

NAME: SAETIA

RIG: Steam Screw

REGISTERED NUMBER: 215965

DATE & LOCATION BUILT: 1918; Bethlehem Shipbuilding
                              Corporation at Wilmington,
                              Delaware

DATE SUNK: November 9, 1918 at 9:05 a.m.

REPORTED POSITION WHERE SUNK: 10 miles southeast of
                              Fenwick Island, Maryland and
                              25 miles off Maryland coast
                              (known as Twin wrecks) in 84'
                              of water

                              38°14'18"N
                              74°44'54"W

MASTER AT TIME OF SINKING: Captain W. S. Lynch of
                              Pleasantville, New Jersey

CARGO AT TIME OF SINKING: ballast

LAST PORT SAILED FROM.   France

PORT BOUND FOR: Philadelphia, Pennsylvania

CONSTRUCTION: 2,873 gross tons; steel;
                              length 309.2'; breadth 48.2';
                              depth 21.5'; 1,600 h.p. engine

OTHER DATA:

Evening Public Ledger
Monday, November 11, 1918

Victims of Mine Saved By Song
Cape May Patrol Crew Hears SAETIA Survivors Sound
Philadelphians Assist
Men Plunge Into Surf and Rescue Hungry and Exhausted Sailors

Fifteen survivors of the United States steamship SAETIA, which was sunk off the New Jersey coast November 9, were rescued early today by patrol crews from the naval base at Cape May.

Despite the fact that they had been in an open boat for nearly forty eight hours and their provisions were limited to a tin of biscuits and water, the morale of the survivors was strong. The singing of the men, all of whom seemed to feel by instinct that "Germany was beaten", led to their discovery.

The entire fifteen will be sent to Philadelphia tonight.

Many of the rescuers who manned the boats were Philadelphia boys, and they were compelled to plunge into a heavy sea to reach the survivors. They were in a famished condition but cheerful and hopeful to the last.

Those rescued follow:

Lieutenant Guy M. Jones, U.S. Army; John J. Penzer, Naval Reserve; Barton A. Swarr, U.S. Navy; George Goldborough, U.S. Navy; Abraham B. Amper, Naval Reserve; Leonard W. Chesley, U.S. Navy; George E. Gess, U.S. Navy; William S. Long, Naval Reserve; James C. Connell, Naval Reserve; John Warwick, Naval Reserve; Fran O. Wanamaker, Naval Reserve; Ralph N. Ungemach, Naval Reserve; Norman J. Griffiths, U.S. Navy; and Fred R. Stuits, Naval Reserve.

It is generally believed that the ship was sunk by a mine, but this cannot be verified as officers of the naval base at Cape May decline to discuss the accident.

Public Ledger
Philadelphia, Sunday Morning, November 10, 1918

Steamship Sunk By Mine; Fate of 20 Uncertain
Saetia, 5000 Tons, Is Wrecked Off Coast of Maryland
Heavy Seas Makes Rescues Difficult
Vessel on Way to Philadelphia After Voyage to France

Washington, Nov. 9 - Information received tonight by the Navy Department indicates all the crew of the American steamship SAETIA escaped before that vessel sank this morning off the Maryland coast, presumably after striking a mine.

Announcement by the department said seven officers and forty men had been landed at Coast Guard Station NO. 146, on the Delaware coast, and that thirty-seven or thirty-eight men, all the remainder of the crew, had got away in boats.

Saetia Sinks Twenty Minutes After Explosion Wrecks the Ship

Ocean City, Md., Nov. 9 - The American steamship SAETIA, bound from a French port for Philadelphia, struck a mine twenty-five miles off the Maryland coast at 9:05 a.m. today and sank twenty minutes later.

Forty-seven of the crew were landed here this afternoon and eighteen were taken off a raft at 9 o'clock tonight by a patrolboat.

The chief engineer, Charles Tournier, of Hartford, Conn., was the only one of the rescued who was injured. His leg was crushed between two lifeboats. One of the patrolboats capsized in the sea, but its occupants were rescued.

Destroyers and Coast Guard boats are searching the vicinity for traces of rafts which may be afloat with the rest of the crew. It is feared that the men on duty in the SAETIA's engine room were killed by one of the explosions.

The sinking of the ship was preceded by an explosion a few minutes after 8 o'clock. A few minutes later two more violent explosions followed. Although the ship was light, having just left an American convoy off the Delaware Capes, she went down within twenty minutes, according to her master, Captain W.S. Lynch, of Pleasantville, N.J., who landed at this place.

Destroyers Rushed to Scene

Coast Guard cutters and a number of destroyers rushed to the aid of the steamship, which submerged before any could come alongside, however.

The SAETIA left its convoy returning from France three days ago and was bound for Philadelphia. Just twenty-five miles off this place she ran into the mine, which sent her quivering from bow to stern. Before the ship could back the first explosion threw half the crew into the sea.

Captain Lynch immediately ordered "all hands on deck," but before lifeboats could be lowered the cold salt water pouring upon the boilers caused the additional explosions. The ship careened violently, settling heavily at the stern. With the water pouring through the shaft alley in the stern, only the bow remained on the surface within fifteen minutes. A few minutes later the ship had settled entirely in about 200 feet of water.

Sailors Carried Down By Suction

Due to the excitement and the short time to put off in the lifeboats, none of the crew could give coherent account of the sinking. It is believed, however, that a number of the sailors were taken down by the suction of the freighter as she made her final plunge.

The first rescue ship, a United States Coast Guard launch, to return capsized in the heavy sea which was running all day. All the men were picked up within a few miles of the shore while hundreds of persons crowded the shore.

It was only with the greatest skill that the larger powerboats could ride out the rough seas, and no person could hope to fight long against it. The destroyers and revenue cutters, however, spent the night patrolling the adjacent waters for any survivors.

Those landed here were scantily clad and fatigued after several hours in the water. Their weakened condition was aggravated by the six hours ride in the small boats, which were like corks on the heavy seas.

The Seaside Hotel has been turned over to the local chapter of the Red Cross by Daniel Trimper. Here the survivors will be fed, clothed and sheltered by the town, with the co-operation of the Red Cross. Among those at the hotel is Captain Lynch, who stood by his ship to the last.

Although it had been rumored that the SAETIA had been torpedoed, naval authorities here scout the idea. The stories related by the crew also tended to disprove it.

NAME: SALAS (British)
(Formerly Musie)

RIG: Brig

DATE & LOCATION BUILT: 1861; Deep River, Connecticut

DATE SUNK: November, 1881

REPORTED POSITION WHERE SUNK: 38° 4'N 74° 4'E

MASTER AT TIME OF SINKING: Captain Oliver

CARGO AT TIME OF SINKING: 10,000 cases of petroleum shipped by J. DeRivera and Company

PORT BOUND FOR: Majorca Island

CONSTRUCTION: 443 tons

OTHER DATA:

November 27, 1881
New York Times
Page 14, Column 3
Wreck of the Spanish Brig

Her Captain and a Sailor Drowned -
Other Disasters at Sea

The German ship Hedwig, Capt. Missen, which arrived from Trieste yesterday, brought nine survivors of the Spanish brig SALAS, which left this port last Tuesday. Capt. Missen gives a thrilling account of the abandonment of the Spanish brig, during which two lives were lost. At 11:30 on Thursday last, while the Hedwig was lying to under sail, a stranger, which proved to be the brig SALAS, was seen showing signals of distress. The Hedwig ran down to her, and found her signaling that she had sprung a leak, and, being in a bad condition, desired the ship to lay by. After a short time the brig showed signals which denoted that the leak was increasing and that she would have to be abandoned. In order to find them a proper amount of room in which to launch their boat, the Hedwig kept away, and when a short distance off backed her yards. When nearly abeam her helm was put hard up, for the brig was coming too near. The ship paid off rapidly, and but for this both vessels would have come together in the trough of the sea. As it was the boom-iron of the brig's foreyard caught the back stays of the ship, and, breaking off, fell on the deck of the latter. The mate and four men belonging to the brig then jumped to the deck of the ship. The Captain could have followed, but seeing that five of his men were still on board her was unwilling to desert them. It had been the intention of all to jump upon the ship together. Capt. Missen kept his vessel away as much as possible. He naturally felt greatly alarmed at the reckless conduct of the Spaniards in attempting to run alongside and jump to his decks, for had the vessels come together heavily the ship as well as the brig might have been lost. The ship soon worked to windward, where it was impossible for the brig to reach her. Capt. Missen then told them to launch their boat, but the sea was very heavy and they hesitated about leaving the wreck. Finally a boat was lowered, and then all seemed to be confusion on the brig. The boat had evidently been swamped, and was seen to float astern. Night was coming on, and as there were prospects of a still heavier storm, Capt. Missen concluded to launch a boat. This made its way almost to the side of the brig. The latter was rolling about in a dangerous manner, and her ropes were flying loosely. There were four men on deck who were unwilling to jump overboard and run the risk of not being fished out of the water by the occupants of the small boat. The latter made signs to the four men to throw a line to them. This was done and the line was made fast around the waist of one of the sailors on the brig, who plunged overboard and was hauled into the boat. The other three survivors were rescued in the same manner, and were dragged into the boat, which, after much difficulty, came alongside the Hedwig, and all reached the deck to safety. The men reported that when the brig's boat was swamped, Capt. Oliver and a seaman names Jose Calap were drowned. The survivors had saved nothing but the clothes which they had on at the time. They abandoned the brig none too soon, for after the rescue the sea became still rougher. The wreck was last seen on Friday morning at 8 o'clock in latitude 38° 4' and longitude 74° 4'. It was then apparently full of water, and was only kept afloat by the cargo in the hold. The SALAS left this port for the Island of Majorca on Tuesday last with a cargo of 19,000 cases of petroleum.

The survivors say that she began to leak during a storm on the following morning, and although the pumps were manned the leak gained steadily. On Thursday morning the brig was filling rapidly, and when the Hedwig was sighted a signal of distress was displayed. The nine survivors were well cared for on the Hedwig. They will be sent to their homes in a short time by the Spanish Consul. The lost cargo of petroleum was shipped by J. De Rivera & Co., of this City, and was valued at $12,000, which was covered by insurance. The brig was worth more, but it is not known whether she was insured. She belonged to Señor Salas, of Palms, Majorca, and measured 443 tons. She was built at Deep River, Conn. in 1861, and was at first called the Music. In 1873, she was thoroughly repaired and sold to Señor Salas, who had her name changed to the SALAS. Capt. Oliver, who was lost, is spoken of as a brave man and a good navigator.

Copyright 1879/1880/1881/1883/1884/1887/1889/1895/1913/1918
by The New York Times Company. Reprinted by permission.

NAME: ST. EUSTATIA (Dutch)

DATE SUNK: December 30, 1783

REPORTED POSITION WHERE SUNK: off Gull Shoals near
                                Assateague

CONSTRUCTION: 410 tons, 26 guns

NAME: SALLIE W. KAY

RIG: Schooner

DATE SUNK: January 10, 1883 at 6:15 A.M.

REPORTED POSITION WHERE SUNK: Fenwick Island, actually
                                80th Street in Ocean City,
                                Maryland (5 miles north of
                                Ocean City Inlet) 1/8 mile off
                                beach

MASTER AT TIME OF SINKING: Captain Smith
                                (8 persons on board; 7 saved -
                                German seaman named Anton was
                                lost)

CARGO AT TIME OF SINKING: coal

LAST PORT SAILED FROM: Baltimore, Maryland

PORT BOUND FOR: Boston, Massachusetts

CONSTRUCTION: 377 tons; 3 masts; 2 decks

OTHER DATA: stranded; crew was rescued by
                                breeches buoy from Ocean City
                                Lifesaving Station under the
                                command of Keeper William West;
                                James Crawford also helped by
                                taking everyone back to station
                                in a wagon along with 12 Ocean
                                City residents

NAME: SALVATORE

RIG: Barge

DATE SUNK: September 10, 1889

REPORTED POSITION WHERE SUNK: 1 mile east of Lewes
                                  Station

MASTER AT TIME OF SINKING: Captain Romain and 9 persons;
                                  all 10 saved

CARGO AT TIME OF SINKING: case oil

HOME PORT: Naples, Italy

LAST PORT SAILED FROM: Philadelphia, Pennsylvania

PORT BOUND FOR: Cagliari, Italy

CONSTRUCTION: 287 tons

NAME: SAMARANG

RIG: Schooner

DATE SUNK: 1826

REPORTED POSITION WHERE SUNK: off Gull Shoals

NAME:	SAN GIL (Panamanian)
RIG:	Freighter
DATE & LOCATION BUILT:	by Workman Clark and Company
DATE SUNK:	February 4, 1942
REPORTED POSITION WHERE SUNK:	38°06'06"N 74°37'00"W 26.5 miles off Winter Quarter Beach, Maryland in 96' of water
CONSTRUCTION:	3,598 tons; 325' long; breadth 46.3'; depth 29.2'; 330 h.p. triple expansion engine
OTHER DATA:	Captain John Steffey, charter boat "Good Time Diver II" knows exact location.

NAME:	SAN LORENZO de ESCORIAL (Spanish)
RIG:	Ship
DATE & LOCATION BUILT:	1807 - 1808; Cuba
DATE SUNK:	September, 1820
REPORTED POSITION WHERE SUNK:	ashore on Assateague Island, Maryland
MASTER AT TIME OF SINKING:	Pedro Ceiza de Fernandez
CARGO AT TIME OF SINKING:	95 ponies; 3,973 gold doubloons, 22,900 pieces of eight dated 1770 to 1817; 255 bars of gold; 303 bars of silver; statue of Madonna from Cathedral of Lima; 13,200 pieces of four; 8,000 pieces of two; 136 passengers (only 2 survived)
LAST PORT SAILED FROM:	Porto Belo, Carribean; July, 1820
PORT BOUND FOR:	Spain
WEATHER CONDITIONS AT TIME OF SINKING:	rain, high southeast winds
CONSTRUCTION:	wood, 28 cannons
OTHER DATA:	She struck a shoal; the wreckage was soon scattered northward along coast. A map of 1835 shows wreckage of a vessel 3 miles below present inlet.

NAME:	SAN MIGUEL
DATE SUNK:	October 3, 1795
REPORTED POSITION WHERE SUNK:	Gull Shoals

NAME: SAN VICENZO FLIORENGO

REGISTERED NUMBER: (Italian)
DATE SUNK: December 27, 1818
REPORTED POSITION WHERE SUNK: Fenwick Shoals
OTHER DATA: foundered

NAME: SANTA ROSALEA (Spanish)

RIG: Merchantman
DATE SUNK: 1788
REPORTED POSITION WHERE SUNK: near Cape Henlopen
MASTER AT TIME OF SINKING: Captain Pardanus
LAST PORT SAILED FROM: Baltimore, Maryland
PORT BOUND FOR: Havana, Cuba

NAME: SANTO CRISTO

REPORTED POSITION WHERE SUNK: Assateague Island

NAME: SANTO LEOCADIA (Portugese)

RIG: Ship
DATE SUNK: 1828
REPORTED POSITION WHERE SUNK: off Fenwick Shoals
CONSTRUCTION: 800 tons

NAME:	SARAH W. LAWRENCE
RIG:	Schooner
REGISTERED NUMBER:	116106; Call Letters KDLM
DATE & LOCATION BUILT:	1886; Bath, Maine by New England Shipbuilding Company
DATE SUNK:	February 10, 1909
REPORTED POSITION WHERE SUNK:	Hen and Chicken Shoal 1,000 yards northwest of "C-3" buoy; N 38°44'40" W 75°03'06" 3/4 mile offshore due east of 3rd concrete watch tower, down from Cape Henlopen
CARGO AT TIME OF SINKING:	coal
HOME PORT:	Fall River, Massachusetts
LAST PORT SAILED FROM:	Newport News, Virginia
PORT BOUND FOR:	Boston, Massachusetts
PHOTOGRAPH &/OR DRAWING:	Mariners Museum Photo PK6442
CONSTRUCTION:	wood; 1,369.76 tons gross; 1,301.28 tons net; 4 masts; length 217.0'; breadth 45.2'; depth 19.8'
OTHER DATA:	wreck is really broken up and scattered; lies in 30' of water on a sandy bottom; extends off bottom 5'; visibility usually poor - 3-1/2' ribs and some planking visible; Captain Robert Byre - charter boat "Adie Mae" and Captain Bill Tattersal - charter boat "Mr. Ike" know exact location

SARAH W. LAWRENCE

Courtesy of the Mariners Museum, Newport News, Virginia 23606

NAME:	SARAH C. PARK
RIG:	Schooner
REGISTERED NUMBER:	23427
DATE & LOCATION BUILT:	1867; Clew's Landing, New Jersey
DATE SUNK:	September 10, 1889
REPORTED POSITION WHERE SUNK:	2 miles north of Rehobeth Station
HOME PORT:	Bridgeton, New Jersey
CONSTRUCTION:	36.09 gross tons; 34.29 net tons; length 62.4'; breadth 22.8'; depth 4.5'
OTHER DATA:	stranded

NAME:	SCORPION
RIG:	Brig
DATE SUNK:	July, 1759
REPORTED POSITION WHERE SUNK:	ashore near Gull Shoals, Assateague Island
CONSTRUCTION:	armed privateer

NAME:	<u>SCULLY</u>
RIG:	Schooner
REGISTERED NUMBER:	115632; Call Letters JTDV
DATE & LOCATION BUILT:	1878; New Castle, Maine
DATE SUNK:	March 30, 1919
REPORTED POSITION WHERE SUNK:	entrance to inner harbor, Delaware
HOME PORT:	Norfolk, Virginia
CONSTRUCTION:	1,542 tons gross; 1,542 tons net; length 216.0'; breadth 40.1'; depth 24.4'

NAME:	<u>SEA BIRD</u>
RIG:	Schooner
REGISTERED NUMBER:	23777; Call Letters JGSD
DATE & LOCATION BUILT:	1869; Tuckahoe, New Jersey
DATE SUNK:	September 16, 1903
REPORTED POSITION WHERE SUNK:	3/4 mile north/northeast of Lewes Station
MASTER AT TIME OF SINKING:	Captain Crowley and 4 persons (all 5 saved)
HOME PORT:	Boston, Massachusetts (formerly Bridgeton, New Jersey)
LAST PORT SAILED FROM:	Hudson River
PORT BOUND FOR:	Hampton, Virginia
CONSTRUCTION:	187.98 gross tons; 163 net tons; length 100.8'; breadth 29.4'; depth 8.1'

NAME:	S.G. WILDER
RIG:	Schooner - barge
REGISTERED NUMBER:	116145
DATE & LOCATION BUILT:	1887; Port Blakely, Washington
DATE SUNK:	July 3, 1933
REPORTED POSITION WHERE SUNK:	Fenwick Island 38° 14'18"N 74° 44'42"W known as Twin Wrecks (see "Fishing Guide to Maryland")
MASTER AT TIME OF SINKING:	5 on board (3 lost)
HOME PORT:	San Francisco, California
CONSTRUCTION:	wood; 604 gross tons; length 166.8'; breadth 37.3'; depth 14.0'
OTHER DATA:	foundered; charter captains from Ocean City know the location of this wreck

NAME:	SINGLETON PALMER
RIG:	Schooner
REGISTERED NUMBER:	Signal Letters KTBH
DATE & LOCATION BUILT:	1904; Waldoboro, Maine by G. L. Weldt
DATE SUNK:	November 6, 1921
REPORTED POSITION WHERE SUNK:	from page 67 of "Great Coal Schooners of Maine" by Parker reports her as being south of 34°08'N; 66°46'W - 60 miles offshore; Lloyd's wreck reports her as 10 miles N E x E of Fenwick Shoal Light
OWNER:	France and Canada Steamship Corporation
MASTER AT TIME OF SINKING:	Captain J. M. Griffin; Mate Swen Lanstron; Seaman Thomas Jones; Deck Engineer Charles Swanson
CARGO AT TIME OF SINKING:	in ballast
LAST PORT SAILED FROM:	Perth Amboy, New Jersey
PORT BOUND FOR:	Norfolk, Virginia
WEATHER CONDITIONS AT TIME OF SINKING	calm
PHOTOGRAPH &/OR DRAWING:	Mariners Museum Photo PK-196
CONSTRUCTION:	wood; 5 masts; 2,859 gross tons; double decks; length 294'; beam 45'; sister ship of Elizabeth Palmer
OTHER DATA:	sunk by collision; the "Apache" steamship struck her just aft of the main rigging; 1 life lost (Charles Swanson); 9 saved

November 7, 1921
Bath Daily Times

Palmer's Survivors Reach Boston With Story of Collision

M. Griffin Describes Thrilling Events After Apache Hits His Ship
and Confirms Loss Engineer Charles Swanson

Boston, November 7 - Reports of the loss of Charles Swanson, engineer of the five masted schooner SINGLETON PALMER, when that schooner was run down by the Clyde liner "Apache" by Fenwick Island lightship yesterday were confirmed by Capt. J. M. Griffin, who with eight other survivors of the schooner came here today on the steamer "Gloucester" which rescued them. Swanson's home was in New York City.

Swanson, according to Capt. Griffin, took refuge in the rigging when the PALMER was struck. The schooner listed sharply to starboard, as the "Apache" backed away, and as the stricken vessel rocked up and down on the waves, Swanson was repeatedly forced under water. Eventually, the captain thought, he was struck by debris and lost his hold. Two other members of the crew, mate Swen Lanstron, and Thomas Jones, seaman, were washed overboard but were picked up by the "Apache" and taken to New York.

His vessel was struck squarely, just aft the main rigging, Capt. Griffin said. The "Apache" then backed away and sent out a small boat, which made two trips, to learn the name of the schooner.

It was starting to return again, Griffin said, when he asked "If they intended to let us all drown." Meanwhile the "Gloucester" arrived and sent a small boat which took off the captain and eight remaining men. The "Gloucester" effected the rescue and was on her way again in 48 minutes.

The loss of the SINGLETON PALMER leaves but two of the once famous PALMER fleet afloat. The "Dorothy Palmer" and the "Rebecca Palmer" alone survive.

The PALMER was owned by the France & Canada Steamship Corporation and was valued at $45,000.

NAME: **SOLON**

RIG: Brig

DATE SUNK: November 9, 1846

REPORTED POSITION WHERE SUNK: near Green Run Inlet

NAME:	SOUTHERN SWORD
RIG:	Steam Screw cut down to barge at time of sinking (conversion in 1937 by Max Rose)
REGISTERED NUMBER:	217267
DATE & LOCATION BUILT:	1918; Superior, Wisconsin by Globe Shipbuilding Company
DATE SUNK:	March 18, 1946
REPORTED POSITION WHERE SUNK:	38° 36'N; 74° 56'W due east of Indian River Inlet 6 miles
OWNER:	Martin Marine Transportation Company of Delaware; 111 Walnut Street, Philadelphia, Pennsylvania
MASTER AT TIME OF SINKING:	(1 man crew)
CARGO AT TIME OF SINKING:	coal
HOME PORT:	Philadelphia, Pennsylvania
LAST PORT SAILED FROM:	Hampton Roads
PORT BOUND FOR:	New York City
WEATHER CONDITIONS AT TIME OF SINKING:	heavy
PHOTOGRAPH &/OR DRAWING:	Mariners Museum Photo 1261
CONSTRUCTION:	steel; 2,180 gross tons; 2,064 net tons; length 251.0'; breadth 43.6'; depth 22.2'
OTHER DATA:	foundered while in tow; the wreck lays in 65' of water; visibility is usually so poor that determination of condition is very difficult; however, much of the ship remains; charter captains from Indian River, Delaware know exact location of this wreck

SOUTHERN SWORD

Courtesy of the Mariners Museum, Newport News, Virginia 23606

NAME: STARLIGHT

RIG: Schooner

DATE SUNK: August 2, 1901

REPORTED POSITION WHERE SUNK: 200 yards north of Rehobeth Beach Station

MASTER AT TIME OF SINKING: Captain Magee and 1 person

CARGO AT TIME OF SINKING: lumber

HOME PORT: Wilmington, Delaware

LAST PORT SAILED FROM: Millville, New Jersey

PORT BOUND FOR: Millville, New Jersey

CONSTRUCTION: 9 tons

NAME STRICKLAND

RIG: Snow

DATE SUNK: Sunday, December 16, 1754

REPORTED POSITION WHERE SUNK: Indian River

MASTER AT TIME OF SINKING: Captain Baker (all persons saved)

CARGO AT TIME OF SINKING: cargo lost

LAST PORT SAILED FROM: West Indies

PORT BOUND FOR: Philadelphia, Pennsylvania

OTHER DATA: vessel beat to pieces at time of sinking

NAME:	U.S.S. S-5 (S.S. 110)
RIG:	Submarine
REGISTERED NUMBER:	U.S. Navy
DATE & LOCATION BUILT:	launched November 20, 1919; Portsmouth Navy Yard Portsmouth, New Hampshire
DATE SUNK:	Wednesday, September 1, 1920
REPORTED POSITION WHERE SUNK:	39°40"00"N; 74°08'00"W in 156' of water; towed to 38°30'N; 74°10'W in 144' of water
OWNER:	U.S. Navy
MASTER AT TIME OF SINKING:	Lieutenant Commander Charles M. Cooke, Jr., Lieutenant Charles Grisham; Ensign J.E. Longstaff; 30 crewmen
CARGO AT TIME OF SINKING:	none; on practice mission shipped by J. DeRivera
HOME PORT:	Boston Navy Yard
LAST PORT SAILED FROM:	Boston, Massachusetts
PORT BOUND FOR:	Baltimore, Maryland
WEATHER CONDITIONS AT TIME OF SINKING:	good
PHOTOGRAPH &/OR DRAWING:	courtesy Captain John Longstaff, U.S.N. (retired)
CONSTRUCTION:	steel; 1,092 tons; length 231'; sister ship S-4
OTHER DATA:	The S-5 foundered because of a failure in air induction during practice dive 55 miles off Cape Henlopen. The crew was rescued by cutting a hole in the stern of the sub which was out of water and signaling a passing ship "Alanthus" and other ship "General Goethals." The battleship "Ohio" came out and began to tow the sub into port but the towing cable parted and she

sank completely. They marked the
site and salvage was attempted
later that month but weather
halted salvage. Ens. Longstaff
assisted in salvage attempt and
is now a Capt. U.S.N. (retired).

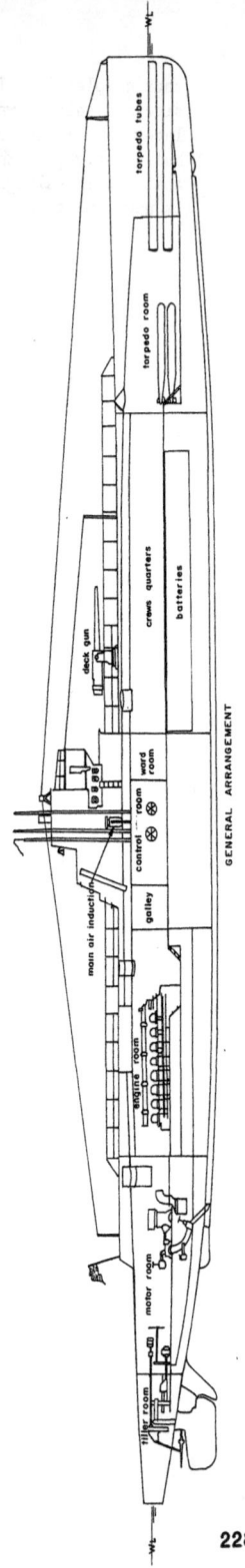

New York Times
Friday, September 5, 1920

Rescuing the Crew Imprisoned Hours in Submarine S-5

Twelve of the Thirty Taken Off and Rest Will be Saved,
According to Wireless Message

In Peril for 42 Hours

Submarine Kept at Surface by Line From Her Stern
to the Transport General Goethals

Naval Vessels Hurried Aid

Men Kept Alive by Air Fed Through Hole Cut Into Hull
of Submerged Vessel

Philadelphia - Sept. 5 - Twelve of the crew of the Submarine S-5 which had been held close to the surface for hours by a line from the United States Army transport General Goethals, after the submarine had become disabled were taken off and the rest were being rescued, according to a wireless message received at 2 o'clock this morning at the Philadelphia Navy Yard from the General Goethals via Cape May.

The first man was taken off at twenty minutes after 10 o'clock when the submarine had been submerged for more than forty-two hours.

Data taken from Admiral Lockwood's book Hell at 50 Fathoms, U.S. Navy files; and Captain John Longstaff, U.S.N. (retired)

Wednesday, September 1, 1920, 1:00 p.m.: The newly commissioned U.S. Submarine S-5 on maneuvers off the coast of Delaware, began a routine practice dive that was to be her last. Lieutenant Commander Charles M. Cooke on the bridge of the S-5 sounded the diving alarm horn twice and followed the men on bridge watch through the tiny conning tower hatch to the control room below. Chief Gunner's twin diesel engines were stopped and disconnected from the shaft clutches. The men in the motor room aft under the direction of Warrant Officer Robert Holt, had already thrown the battery operated main motors on and the sub's propellers were again engaged. Bow plane down, ballast tanks open, the sub began her descent.

Suddenly, Cooke realized that the main air induction valve had not been closed, as water began gushing out of the control room ventilator as well as throughout the ship's ventilation system. Cooke grabbed the induction valve wheel while shouting the order "Surface."

Ballast tank vents were immediately closed; the forward and middle main ballast and safety tanks were blown, and the diving rudders turned to hard rise.

Chief Fox, Lieutenant Grisham and Cooke tried with all their strength to turn the induction valve wheel, but the force of the incoming sea was too much. Finally, with the aid of a large monkey wrench they managed to close the valve, but not tight. Despite all efforts, the sub continued to dive, striking the bottom and throwing the crew off their feet.

Meanwhile, the water entering the engine room had shorted out one main motor while, throughout the ship, electrical circuits were sparking like a fireworks display. Flooding in the forward torpedo room forced evacuation aft into the battery compartment.

As the situation began to settle down, Cooke went on an inspection tour of the ship to determine what exact course of action to take next. He realized communication with the outside world was impossible and it might be days before anyone would find or rescue them.

Examining the water tight integrity of the ship, while looking at the damage done by the water already in the forward compartments assured Cooke that even though the sub had suffered considerable internal damage, her hull was still watertight. Everyone had kept calm and stayed at their posts without panic in the true tradition of submariners. Even Ensign John Longstaff, who was just out of the Academy of Annapolis, remained at his station by the gyrocompass.

You can imagine the thoughts of all the crew during the events up to now. The sub was lying on a mud bottom in 170 feet of water 40 miles off the Delaware coast completely cut off from the world at the surface of the sea. What had started as a routine practice dive was to become one of the most determined and heroic escapes from a disabled submarine!

When Cooke realized from the depth gauge reading, that she lay in 170 feet he decided that since the sub was 231 feet in length he might be able to expel enough water to raise her stern to the surface. By blowing the after main ballast tank the ship might lift enough to move all the water still in the motor, engine and control rooms forward to the battery room. This could prove to be disasterous however, as when sea water mixes with sulfuric acid from the batteries, deadly chlorine gas forms. Also, there was a possibility that the bow might not be able to support the weight of the sub as she would practically be "standing on her nose."

The order for the after main ballast tank to be blown was given. Slowly, very slowly, the stern began to lift. Water began to flow forward through the compartments, spilling over the door sills in a gradual movement to the battery room.

Suddenly, the stern rose sharply sending tons of sea water cascading through the ship in a forward journey along with every piece of loose gear. Men and equipment were washed into the battery room and the water tight door between the control room and the engine room slammed shut. With all the sea water in the battery room, chlorine gas began to form so the men had to get out quickly. But how?

The passageway out was high above their heads, as the ship was nearly vertical. They were also swimming about trying to stay afloat.

Longstaff acted quickly! Tearing the wardroom curtains down, he made sort of a rope to pull them up out of the battery room, rapidly filling with chlorine gas and water.

When everyone was safely in the control room the battery room door was dogged tight and the crew began to work on the door into the engine room, now overhead, which would make it possible for them to move farther aft into the engine and motor rooms with the rest of the crew.

Finally the entire crew, 33 men and 4 officers, huddled in the engine and motor rooms. Cooke then took Chief Bender, Chief Machinist mates Fred W. Whitehead, and Russel Hutson and worked his way back into the tiller room. Cookes' theory was that the very stern would be out of water since the depth of water was only 170 feet and the length of the sub being 231 feet.

Tapping on the hull they soon discovered that possibly about 25 feet of her was above the surface. A breast drill was handed up with a 1/8 inch bit and the laborous task of drilling a hole through 3/4 inch plate steel began. As the bit broke through, the men watched anxiously to see if water or air poured through.

How welcome was the air flowing in that tiny hole! Cooke turned to his men to tell them the first good news since they nosed into the bottom, seven hours before.

The next problem that lay ahead was multi-faceted! A hole, large enough for a man to pass through, had to be formed using hand tools, with the greatest speed possible, so that the remaining oxygen in the sub was not used up before the carbon dioxide, exhaled by the 37 men, killed them all.

The power drill proved to be more of a torture tool than a life-saving instrument. Circuits were badly grounded and the men working in soaking wet clothing were subjected to electrical currents passing through their bodies. The electricity gave out after while and the men were forced to make do with hand tools in complete darkness.

For 30 hours the men of the S-5 drilled, sawed, chiseled and hammered away at that tiny opening until on Thursday, September 2nd, the hole measured a mere 6 inches by 5 inches. The men were near exhaustion now but no one complained as each took his turn making that escape hole larger. It had been thought that the hole might improve the air situation, but it seemed worse.

A long length of pipe with a shirt was raised out of this little hole in hopes that a passing ship might see it.

At last a ship appeared and Cooke waved the makeship flag wildly until
she came quite close, close enough that you could yell. But the ship
suddenly passed out of view! You can imagine the disappointment those
men shared. Frantically they looked about for a dry match or something
to ignite a torch, thinking that a smoke signal would surely bring that
ship back. Nothing! No method could be found to ignite a rag, so they
wearily resumed their task of making the hole larger.

Suddenly, the same ship, a small wood freighter, that had been sighted
before, came back into view, this time coming to a stop nearby. Someone
called out from the freighter and immediately Cooke answered. A boat
lowered from the freighter came over to the submarine and the following
conversations, taken from Naval records and the book Hell at 50 Fathoms,
took place:

Captain of the freighter: "Captain Edward Johnson of steamer Alanthus,
What ship is this?"

Cooke: "The submarine S-5, U.S. Navy."

Johnson, in a demanding tone: "Who is speaking?"

Cooke replied: "Lieutenant Commander Charles M. Cooke, commanding."

Johnson: "What is your destination?"

Cooke, hearing this last question, didn't know what to make of his
rescuer's persistent questioning. His sense of humor phrased the
answer: "Hell, by compass!"

Johnson now offered his help. Not a moment too soon, either, as the low
oxygen level aboard the sub along with the temperature of those tiny
compartments being in excess of $120°$ had drained the men completely. All
food and water had been consumed long ago.

The Alanthus quickly rigged a hose to pump fresh air into that little
hole, while fresh water, by the buckets, was funneled into the crew.

Cables from the Alanthus were lashed around the stern of the S-5 to
assure the upright stability of her.

Soon signals of distress raised by the freighter had brought the Pan-
American liner George W. Goethals to the scene, which, in turn, radioed
the Navy. Responding, the battleship Ohio, along with other naval
ships, steamed towards the site. In the meantime, the drilling,
hammering and chiseling continued. On Friday, September 3rd, 3:34 a.m.,
Cooke, the last man traditionally to leave his ship, dogged the tiller
room door and exited through the hole.

Dawn that morning saw the Ohio, along with the U.S.S. Mallard, standing by, making preparations for towing the stricken sub the 40 miles to the capes. The sub must have really been jammed into the mud for it took a lot of pulling to break her loose. Finally, the slow journey into port began with the sub in tow, but the weather turned foul, and with high seas running, the 6 inch towing cable parted allowing the S-5 to go to the bottom. Buoys were placed, marking her location, with the intent of sending salvage ships to the site as soon as the weather cleared.

U.S.S. Beaver and the U.S.S. Mallard were ordered to make the first investigations into salvaging the S-5, which now lay on her port side, bow pointing east, hard sand bottom, in 150 feet of water, 35 miles due east of Cape Henlopen.

The first divers to descend on her experienced a lot of current and did not complete a full examination of the sub. As winter approached, salvage attempts were haulted until spring, when the U.S.S. Falcon resumed the operation. By August, however, it was apparent that the U.S.S. S-5 would never again rise to sail the surface of the sea. The sub was finally sealed off and the following memo issued:

August 28, 1921

From: Secretary of the Navy

To: Chief of Bureau of Construction and Repair

Subject: U.S.S. S-5 Salvage

1. In view of the recommendations contained herein, salvage operations on Submarine S-5 will be discontinued.

2. Submarine S-5 is considered abandoned this date. The Bureau of Navigation will issue the necessary orders for striking the vessel from the Navy List.

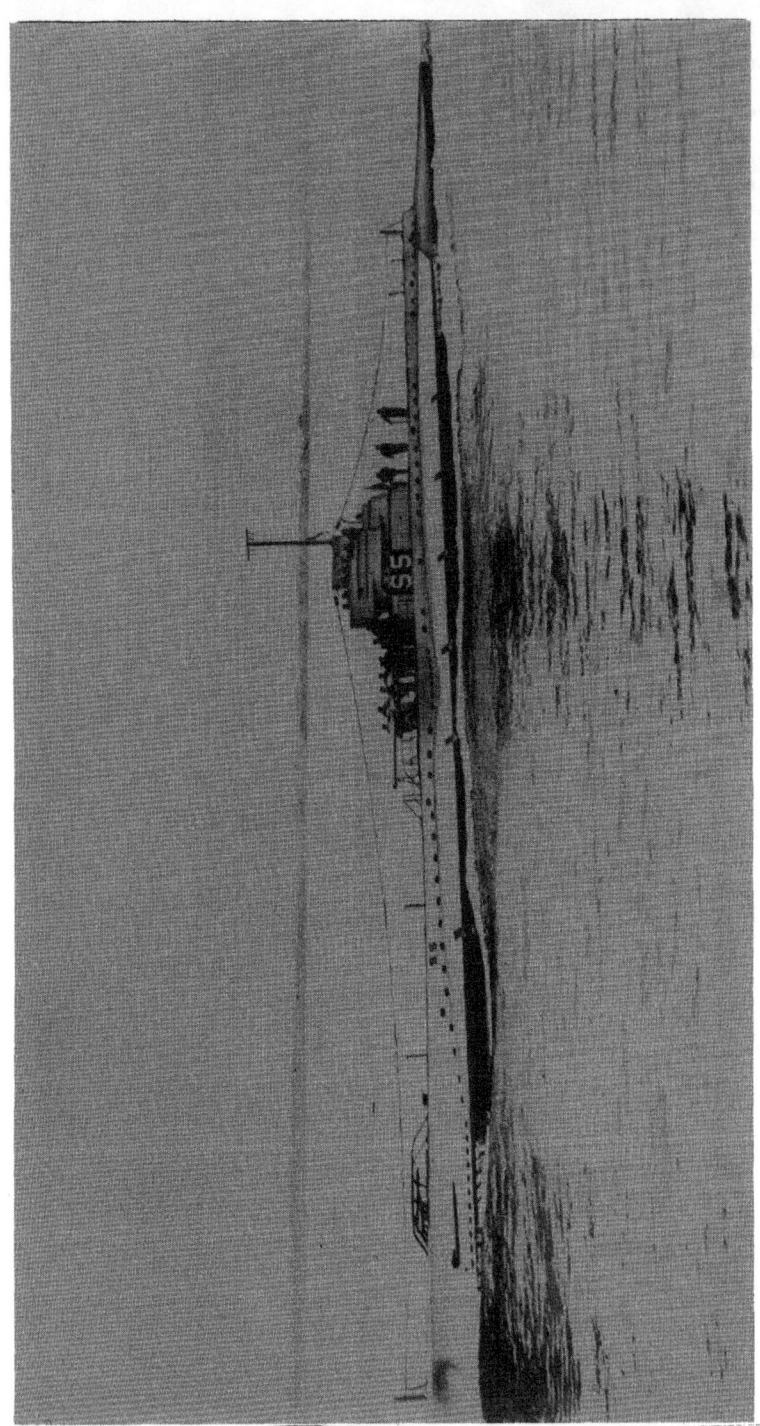

U.S.S. S-5

Courtesy of the United States Navy

NAME:	SUNBURY
RIG:	Schooner - barge
REGISTERED NUMBER:	116898
DATE & LOCATION BUILT:	1899
DATE SUNK:	August 17, 1910 (p.m.)
REPORTED POSITION WHERE SUNK:	5 miles east of Rehobeth Beach life saving station; reportedly 25' of her masts were above water
OWNER:	Staples Coal Company
MASTER AT TIME OF SINKING:	Captain O. Mathewson and 3 persons (all persons saved)
CARGO AT TIME OF SINKING:	coal
HOME PORT:	Fall River, Massachusetts
LAST PORT SAILED FROM:	Hampton Roads, Virginia
PORT BOUND FOR:	Providence, Rhode Island
WEATHER CONDITIONS AT TIME OF SINKING:	E.N.E. wind (fresh); cloudly 70°F.; ebb tide; rough seas
CONSTRUCTION:	1,544 gross tons; 1,419 net tons
OTHER DATA:	supposedly barge struck shoal while in tow of the tug "Waltham"

NAME: SUNRISE

RIG: Barge

REGISTERED NUMBER: 22830

DATE & LOCATION BUILT: 1860; Boston, Massachusetts

DATE SUNK: April 6, 1889

REPORTED POSITION WHERE SUNK: 5 miles N x E from Delaware Breakwater; also "Brown's Shoal" in Delaware Bay

OWNER: Morse Transportation Company of New York

MASTER AT TIME OF SINKING: Captain Harns (5 lives lost)

CARGO AT TIME OF SINKING: coal (1,800 tons)

HOME PORT: New York

LAST PORT SAILED FROM: Norfolk, Virginia

PORT BOUND FOR: Boston, Massachusetts

CONSTRUCTION: wood; 1,184.88 tons gross; 1,125.84 tons net

OTHER DATA: Captain Harnes, wife, 2 small children, and a seaman were all lost; in tow of tug "R.W. Morse"; Joseph Coyle saved

Monday, April 8, 1889
<u>New York Times</u>
Barge Lost With Five Lives

Philadelphia, April 7. - The barge SUNRISE with a cargo of 1,800 tons of coal, went down last night in the Delaware Bay, and the Captain and his wife and their two small children and a seaman were lost. Joseph Coyle, another seaman, drifted about all night in a small boat and was picked up on the beach at Lewes in an almost lifeless condition by one of the life-saving crew.

The SUNRISE left Norfolk Thursday afternoon for New York in tow of the tug-boat R.W. Morse. When off Barnegat yesterday morning the wind was blowing a gale from the northeast, and the Captain decided to put into the Delaware Breakwater. He went up the bay as far as Brown Shoals. This is one of the most dangerous shoals in Delaware Bay, and vessels which anchor near there usually go well over toward the eastern side of the channel. Either the Captain did not know this or else he mistook his bearings in the fog, for he dropped his anchor close to the bell buoy and the tugboat left the barge and went down to the breakwater, a distance of nine miles.

During the night the wind increased in force, and about midnight the Captain found the vessel was dragging her anchors. Finally one of the chains parted and the heavily-laden barge drifted down upon the dangerous shoal. She began to leak so rapidly that the Captain launched the skiff. Coyle slid down the ropes and cast off the hooks. While the Captain was trying to hand Coyle the oars a huge wave lifted the skiff on its crest and the painter parted with a snap. As Coyle drifted astern, he saw the Captain run forward as though to launch the other boat, and then the vessel gave a sudden lurch and seemed to go to pieces. Coyle saw nothing more of the barge.

The SUNRISE was formerly the clipper ship of that name and was owned by the Morse Transportation Company of New York.

Copyright 1879/1880/1881/1883/1884/1887/1889/1895/1913/1918
by The New York Times Company. Reprinted by permission.

NAME: **S.S. SUTTON**

RIG: Steamer, Screw schooner

DATE & LOCATION BUILT: 1897; Port Glasgow by A. Rodger

DATE SUNK: January 20, 1900 (Saturday) stranded at 6:00 a.m.

REPORTED POSITION WHERE SUNK: Fenwick Island Shoal known as "offshore wreck"

OWNER: Sutton S.S. Company (J. Sunley and Co. managers)

MASTER AT TIME OF SINKING: Captain Johnson

CARGO AT TIME OF SINKING: iron ore

HOME PORT: London

LAST PORT SAILED FROM: Carthagena, Spain

PORT BOUND FOR: Philadelphia, Pennsylvania

WEATHER CONDITIONS AT TIME OF SINKING: fog, W.S.W. breeze gentle, cloudy, moderate swell

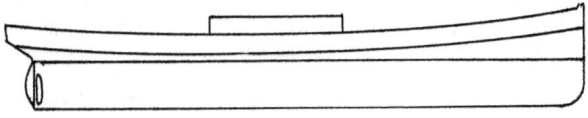

CONSTRUCTION: steel; 2,526 tons; 314.0'0" long; 44.1'1" wide; 20'7" depth; triple expansion engine; 22-1/2"; 37"x61" stroke 42"; 1 deck (steel); two tiers of open beams and deep framing spar deck vessel; water ballast; five bulkheads; steel boiler; main boiler; pressure 160 lbs; engine built by Hall-Brown, Btry. & Company; Glasgow

OTHER DATA: crew was rescued by C.G.C. Onondaga Capt. O.C. Hamlet 12:30 a.m. on January 21; numerous charter boat captains from Indian River Inlet and Ocean City know the exact location of the wrecks on Fenwick Shoals

From the log book of:

U.S.C.G.C. Onondaga (Revenue cutter) Captain O.C. Hamlet

January 20, 1900, Saturday

7:45 p.m. - saw rockets coming up out of fog from Fenwick Island Shoal; W.S.W. breeze, gentle, cloudy, moderate swell, fog lifting

9-1/2 fathoms near ship on Shoals - sent officer in whale boat to investigate S.S. SUTTON, London

Captain Johnson from Carthagena, Spain for Philadelphia, iron ore

She had struck the shoal at 5 a.m., backed off, struck again and bow had sunk in 30' of water, stern still floating but settling, wreck lay outside of whistle buoy.

Took on board Patrick Deven, H. Seymour, A. Mitchell, H. Chester; 19 remaining on board the wreck at their boats - already lowered and ready for use.

11:55 p.m. steamed within one mile of wreck and anchored.

Sunday, January 21

12:30 a.m. rest of 19 persons brought aboard

NAME	<u>TALBOT</u>
RIG:	Schooner - barge
REGISTERED NUMBER:	221405; Signal Letters KNZH
DATE & LOCATION BUILT:	1921; Stratford, Connecticut
DATE SUNK:	October 28, 1938
REPORTED POSITION WHERE SUNK:	Delaware Breakwater
OWNER:	(American) P. Doughterty and Company (Maryland) Hearst Tower Building
HOME PORT:	Baltimore, Maryland
CONSTRUCTION:	wood; 3 masts; 2,229 tons gross; 2,146 tons net; length 267.3'; breadth 46.0'; depth 23.6'
OTHER DATA:	burned; also reported as drifting ashore at Philadelphia

NAME	TECUMSEH
RIG:	Schooner (fore and aft rig)
REGISTERED NUMBER:	Call Letters KGDM
DATE & LOCATION BUILT:	1889 by A. Sewell and Company; Bath, Maine
DATE SUNK:	March 2, 1892
REPORTED POSITION WHERE SUNK:	Fenwick Island Shoals
MASTER AT TIME OF SINKING:	11 persons on board (11 lost)
CARGO AT TIME OF SINKING:	coal
LAST PORT SAILED FROM:	Newport News, Virginia via Baltimore February 18, 1892
PORT BOUND FOR:	Boston, Massachussetts
CONSTRUCTION:	4 masts; 1,658 tons; length 236.1'; breadth 47'; depth 21.4'
OTHER DATA:	stranded

NAME: TENA A. COTTON

RIG: Schooner

REGISTERED NUMBER: 145354; Call Letters KBTH

DATE & LOCATION BUILT: 1883 by C.C. Davidson; Milton, Delaware

DATE SUNK: February 4, 1907

REPORTED POSITION WHERE SUNK: Ocean City, Maryland 4 miles south of Ocean City Station

MASTER AT TIME OF SINKING: Captain Primrose and 6 persons (all 7 saved)

CARGO AT TIME OF SINKING: pilings

HOME PORT: Primrose, New Jersey (Bridgeton, New Jersey, 1904)

LAST PORT SAILED FROM: Norfolk, Virginia

PORT BOUND FOR: New York City

CONSTRUCTION: 3 masts; 377 tons gross; 321 tons net; length 138.8'; breadth 34.2'; depth 10.5'; white oak; yellow pine; galvanized iron fastenings

NAME THADDEUS

RIG: Schooner

DATE SUNK: May 19, 1846

REPORTED POSITION WHERE SUNK: Lewes, Delaware on ice breaker in 26' of water

CARGO AT TIME OF SINKING: 160 tons of coal

PORT BOUND FOR: New York

WEATHER CONDITIONS AT TIME OF SINKING: gale

NAME: THOMAS TRACY
(in service of U.S. Coast Guard)

RIG: Steam screw

REGISTERED NUMBER: Lloyd's Registry No. 86286

DATE & LOCATION BUILT: 1916

DATE SUNK: September 14, 1944; 3:30 p.m.

REPORTED POSITION WHERE SUNK: 100 yards off Rehobeth Beach
38°42'N; 75°04'W

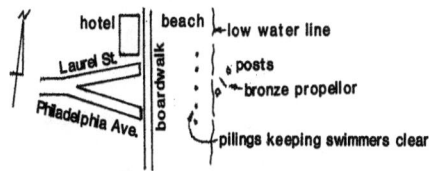

OWNER: U.S. Coast Guard

MASTER AT TIME OF SINKING: 31 crew members rescued by breeches bouy tied to telephone poles

CARGO AT TIME OF SINKING: in ballast

LAST PORT SAILED FROM: New England

PORT BOUND FOR: New England

WEATHER CONDITIONS
AT TIME OF SINKING: hurricane; winds 90 mph

PHOTOGRAGH &/OR DRAWING: U.S. Coast Guard Photo
No. PB 10240

CONSTRUCTION: steel; 300 tons

THOMAS TRACY

NAME: THREE BROTHERS

RIG: Ship (English)

DATE SUNK: reported as 1775 (August 16)

REPORTED POSITION WHERE SUNK: attempting to enter Indian
                                   River Inlet:
                                   33°88'00"N; 75°03'00"W

CARGO AT TIME OF SINKING: 300 immigrants (over 250 were
                                   lost)and 5,000 newly minted
                                   gold rose guineas (King George
                                   III) all dated 1775

PORT BOUND FOR: Philadelphia, Pennsylvania

WEATHER CONDITIONS
AT TIME OF SINKING: hurricane

CONSTRUCTION: 512 tons

NAME: TIMOUR

RIG: Ship

REGISTERED NUMBER: 24094; Call Letters HRQC

DATE & LOCATION BUILT: 1866; Newburyport, Massachusetts

DATE SUNK: September 10, 1889

REPORTED POSITION WHERE SUNK: 1/3 mile west of Lewes Station

MASTER AT TIME OF SINKING: Captain Winters and 5 persons
                                   (all 6 saved)

HOME PORT: Boston, Massachusetts

LAST PORT SAILED FROM: Boston, Massachusetts

PORT BOUND FOR: Norfolk, Virginia

CONSTRUCTION: 962.92 tons gross; length 163.6';
                                   breadth 35.0'; depth 22.8'

NAME:	<u>T.J. HOOPER</u>
RIG:	Schooner - barge
REGISTERED NUMBER:	222353; Call Letters KNZG
DATE & LOCATION BUILT:	1918; Morehead City, North Carolina
DATE SUNK:	January 23, 1935
REPORTED POSITION WHERE SUNK:	off Delaware Coast
OWNER:	Eastern Transportation Company, Delaware; Ford Building
CARGO AT TIME OF SINKING:	coal
HOME PORT:	Wilmington, Delaware
LAST PORT SAILED FROM:	Norfolk, Virginia
PORT BOUND FOR:	New York
CONSTRUCTION:	wood; 2,197 tons gross; 2,114 tons net; length 267.3'; breadth 46.0'; depth 23.6'

NAME: T. MORRIS PEROT

RIG: Schooner

REGISTERED NUMBER: 145072; Signal Letters JRFV

DATE & LOCATION BUILT: August 1875; Jamestown, Virginia

DATE SUNK: September 28, 1913

REPORTED POSITION WHERE SUNK: off Fenwick Island

MASTER AT TIME OF SINKING: Captain William F. Randolph

CARGO AT TIME OF SINKING: in ballast

HOME PORT: New York

LAST PORT SAILED FROM: New York

PORT BOUND FOR: York River, Virginia

CONSTRUCTION: wood; 3 masts; single deck; 310.31 tons gross; 253 tons net; length 124.3'; breadth 33.8'; depth 10.2'

NAME: TWO BROTHERS

RIG: Schooner

DATE SUNK: October 22, 1845

REPORTED POSITION WHERE SUNK: on the bay side of the Delaware Breakwater

CARGO AT TIME OF SINKING: coal

LAST PORT SAILED FROM: Philadelphia, Pennsylvania

PORT BOUND FOR: New Haven

OTHER: insured in Hartford, Connecticut

NAME: URANUS

RIG: Steam packet

DATE SUNK: May 10, 1887

REPORTED POSITION WHERE SUNK: 1-3/4 miles north of
                               Rehobeth Beach Coast Guard
                               Station

MASTER AT TIME OF SINKING: Captain Neimann, Raystock,
                               Germany (16 lives saved)

CARGO AT TIME OF SINKING: iron, rags and barrels

LAST PORT SAILED FROM: Hamburg, Germany

PORT BOUND FOR: Philadelphia, Pennsylvania

CONSTRUCTION: 969 tons

OTHER: vessel was a total loss; she
                               stranded on beach; surfboat
                               was used to remove crew

NAME: VESTAS

RIG: Tug

REPORTED POSITION WHERE SUNK: 6 miles off Indian River
                               Inlet

NAME: WALTER

RIG: Ship

DATE SUNK: October 21, 1844; 5 a.m.

REPORTED POSITION WHERE SUNK: Baltimore Hundred near Indian River, Delaware ashore

MASTER AT TIME OF SINKING: Captain Boyd (pilot Captain Clampett)

HOME PORT: Philadelphia, Pennsylvania

LAST PORT SAILED FROM: Liverpool, England

PORT BOUND FOR: Philadelphia, Pennsylvania

WEATHER CONDITIONS AT TIME OF SINKING: fresh easterly wind

CONSTRUCTION: wood

OTHER DATA: grounded; hull broken up on beach at time of wreck

NAME:	WASHINGTONIAN
RIG:	Steam screw; refrigerated cargo vessel
REGISTERED NUMBER:	211887; Call Letters LDHW; Contract Hull No. 131, Bethlehem Shipyard, Baltimore, Maryland
DATE & LOCATION BUILT:	1914 by Maryland Steel Company at Bethlehem Shipyward
DATE SUNK:	January 26, 1915, 3:40 a.m. (Tuesday); collision with Schooner "Elizabeth Palmer"; 1 life lost - H. Meyer, water tender
REPORTED POSITION WHERE SUNK:	12 miles offshore Fenwick Island, Delaware; Old Dominion Line Steamer "Hamilton" picked up the crews from both ships
	Due magnetic North of whistle buoy "R-2" in 90' of water; Lat. 38°25'46"N Long. 74°46'06"W
OWNER:	American-Hawaiian Lines 90 Broad Street New York (out of business around 1956)
MASTER AT TIME OF SINKING:	Captain Broadhead
CARGO AT TIME OF SINKING:	raw sugar - 10,000 tons
HOME PORT:	New York
LAST PORT SAILED FROM:	Panama Canal
PORT BOUND FOR:	Philadelphia, Pennsylvania
WEATHER CONDITIONS AT TIME OF SINKING:	clear, north/northwest moderate breeze
PHOTOGRAPH &/OR DRAWING:	Photograph - Mariner's Museum, Newport News, Virginia - draft of main deck and outboard profile by R. Moale filed at Mariner's Museum and list of plans retained at Bethlehem Steel Shipyard

CONSTRUCTION:	6,648 tons; length 414'; beam 53.6'; steel hull and main deck oak planks on cabin house and bridge; teakwood trim; brass hardware
OTHER DATA:	30' of bow from stem aft lies directly upside down and extends off the sand about 30' high. Remaining wreckage lays on side. Masts are fairly intack, but weather deck and superstructure have deteriorated. Superstructure is separate from main wreckage. Fantail is fairly intack. Removal of name off port side was accomplished in 1975 by diving club Atlantis Rangers. Visibility on wreck is usually between 20' and 30' extending to 80' under good conditions. A few lobster remain, but mostly deep into wreck. Flounder and Tautog are plentiful and wreck has an abundance of sea anemones and starfish.
	Captains out of Indian River Inlet and Ocean City, Maryland know exact location.

Philadelphia Public Ledger
January 27, 1915

BIG STEAMER SUNK; HIT BY SCHOONER
53 Saved, One Drowned, in Crash Off the Delaware Coast

NEW YORK, Jan. 26. - In a collision near the Fenwick Shoals Lightship early today the American-Hawaiian Line freight steamship WASHINGTONIAN was sunk and the American schooner ELIZABETH PALMER, which rammed her, was abandoned with decks awash. One life was lost, that of a water tender. The other 53 persons comprising the officers and crews of the two vessels were landed in New York tonight by the Old Dominion Line steamer HAMILTON, from Norfolk, which picked them up about 20 miles southwest of the Delaware Breakwater.

A dispatch from Delaware Breakwater late tonight said that the ELIZABETH PALMER was afloat and in an easy position.

The WASHINGTONIAN sank within 10 minutes after the schooner struck her. H. Meyer, a water tender on the WASHINGTONIAN, was missing when the men were mustered for rollcall on the decks of the rescuing ship.

According to Captain George A. Carlisle, who was in command of the schooner, the accident happened about 3:30 a.m. He said:

"It was evident that the steamer was moving in a direction that would have taken her across our bows and that our lights were seen too late to avoid us. We struck the WASHINGTONIAN head-on, making a hole in her almost amidships, the force of the impact smashing in the bow of the schooner. We broke away, and went ahead about a mile before our course was checked. We saw the WASHINGTONIAN go down after remaining afloat for about 10 minutes. While there was a heavy sea running, the wind was comparatively light and only a light haze in the air. Thirteen men and one woman, the wife of John Andres, the steward, were aboard. We took to the lifeboats as soon as our decks were awash and were picked up two hours later by the HAMILTON, which had responded to the wireless calls for assistance sent out by the WASHINGTONIAN."

The steamship WASHINGTONIAN was bound from Honolulu for this port with a cargo of about 8500 tons of raw sugar, valued at more than $1,000,000. This vessel is new, having been completed at the Maryland Steel Company at Sparrows Point, Md., early in 1914. It had a net register of 4046 tons and a carrying capacity of about 8500 tons. It was 407.7 feet long, and was one of the finest and most modern cargo-carrying vessels under the American flag.

WASHINGTONIAN

Courtesy of the Mariners Museum, Newport News, Virginia 23606

NAME: WESTERN BELLE

RIG: Schooner - barge
                                   originally built as a bark rig

REGISTERED NUMBER: 80577

DATE & LOCATION BUILT: 1876 by Goss & Sayer
                                   Bath, Maine

DATE SUNK: Sunday, September 23, 1917
                                   8:00 a.m.

REPORTED POSITION WHERE SUNK: Fenwick Island, Delaware
                                   about 10 miles north of Fenwick
                                   Island Light Station (also
                                   reported as 22 miles east of
                                   Fenwick Station)

OWNER: Neptune Line, Inc.
                                   184 Henderson Street
                                   Jersey City, New Jersey 07302
                                   (212) 943-5534

MASTER AT TIME OF SINKING: Harry Schmidt
                                   62 Saratoga Street
                                   Providence, Rhode Island

CARGO AT TIME OF SINKING: bituminous coal 1,662 tons

HOME PORT: New York, New York

LAST PORT SAILED FROM: Hampton Roads, Virginia
                                   September 21, 1917

PORT BOUND FOR: Providence, Rhode Island

WEATHER CONDITIONS
AT TIME OF SINKING: strong northeast wind, heavy seas

PHOTOGRAPH &/OR DRAWING: Mariners Museum Photo No. PK-26

CONSTRUCTION: wood; no engine; 1,097 gross tons;
                                   1,071 net tons (also listed as
                                   1,124 tons)

OTHER DATA: Vessel carried 4 persons at time
                                   of sinking. Three were lost:
                                   Harry Schmidt, his wife, and
                                   George Haggerty. Vessel was
                                   insured for $4,600. Foundered
                                   while in tow of tug.

WESTERN BELLE

Courtesy of the Mariners Museum, Newport News, Virginia 23606

NAME: WHITE BAND

RIG: Schooner - barge
REGISTERED NUMBER: 140370; Call Letters J.T.L.N.
DATE & LOCATION BUILT: 1879; Kennebunk, Maine
DATE SUNK: January 24, 1908
REPORTED POSITION WHERE SUNK: Cape Henlopen
MASTER AT TIME OF SINKING: 6 persons aboard - all lost
CARGO AT TIME OF SINKING: coal
HOME PORT: Perth Amboy, New Jersey
LAST PORT SAILED FROM: Newport News, Virginia
PORT BOUND FOR: Providence, Rhode Island
CONSTRUCTION: wood; 1,816 gross tons; 1,730 net tons; length 224.3'; breadth 42.1'; depth 18.7
OTHER DATA: foundered

NAME: WM. G. BARTLETT

RIG: Schooner
DATE SUNK: March 12, 1888
REPORTED POSITION WHERE SUNK: Cape Henlopen - Delaware Breakwater
MASTER AT TIME OF SINKING: (1 person lost)
CARGO AT TIME OF SINKING: wood
LAST PORT SAILED FROM: James River, Virginia
PORT BOUND FOR: New York City
CONSTRUCTION: 219 tons

NAME: WILLIAM H. DAVIDSON

RIG: Schooner

REGISTERED NUMBER: 81477; Call Letters KMBC

DATE AND LOCATION BUILT: 1894; New London, Connecticut

DATE SUNK: March 26, 1903

REPORTED POSITION WHERE SUNK: 2-1/2 miles south of Indian River Inlet Station

MASTER AT TIME OF SINKING: Captain Maxwell and 3 persons (all 4 saved)

CARGO AT TIME OF SINKING: lumber

LAST PORT SAILED FROM: Suffolk, Virginia

PORT BOUND FOR: New York City

CONSTRUCTION: 286 tons gross; 272 net tons; length 122.0'; breadth 32.5'; depth 11.2'

NAME: **WILLIAM ELLISON**

RIG: Schooner

REGISTERED NUMBER: 81156

DATE AND LOCATION BUILT: 1887; Rehobeth, Delaware

DATE SUNK: September 10, 1902

REPORTED POSITION WHERE SUNK: near Indian River Inlet

MASTER AT TIME OF SINKING: Captain Lathbery and 1 person (both saved)

CARGO AT TIME OF SINKING: boxes

HOME PORT: Wilmington, Delaware

LAST PORT SAILED FROM: Millville, Delaware

PORT BOUND FOR: Mad Horse Creek

CONSTRUCTION: 16 tons gross; 15 tons net; length 39.5'; breadth 15.0'; depth 3.9

NAME: WILLIAM HALES

RIG: Bark (American)

DATE AND LOCATION BUILT: 1877; Newburyport, Massachusetts

DATE SUNK: November 8, 1895

REPORTED POSITION WHERE SUNK: Latitude 38°; Longitude 74°19'

MASTER AT TIME OF SINKING: Captain Coombs

CARGO AT TIME OF SINKING: old iron

HOME PORT: New York

LAST PORT SAILED FROM: Havana, Cuba

PORT BOUND FOR: Philadelphia, Pennsylvania

WEATHER CONDITIONS
AT TIME OF SINKING: fog

CONSTRUCTION: 834 tons

OTHER DATA:

New York Times
November, 1895
Mariners of Ill-Fated WILLIAM HALES and Ocean Lily Arrive on the Ward Line Steamer Santiago

The Ward Line Steamer Santiago arrived last evening at Quarantine from Nassau and ports on the south side of Cuba with thirty-eight passengers, twenty-six of whom were seamen, some returning home after completing cruises, others shipwrecked mariners.

Seven of the shipwrecked mariners were Capt. Coombs, the mate, Kimmittee, and Seamen Beular, Neilson, Oerlan, Nelson, and Benenduck of the American bark WILLIAM HALES, which was sunk in collision with the Ward Line Steamer Niagara on Friday, November 8, during a dense fog.

Capt. Coombs' story of the disaster is that he sailed from Havana October 27 for Philadelphia with a cargo of old iron. On the morning of November 8, in latitude 38 degrees longitude 74.19, the bark was moving slowly through the water, a dense fog prevailing at the time, when a steamer loomed up suddenly and ran the bark down, cutting her to the water's edge and sinking her immediately.

Capt. Coombs and several of the crew were carried down by the suction of the water, but he with two others came to the surface. Four, who were on deck at the time of the collision, managed to scramble on board of the steamer. Five, who were below sank with the unfortunate vessel. Those lost were Coleman, the second mate; Barnes, the steward, and three seamen - Frank Nevis and two others unknown. The Niagara was not damaged by the collision. She steamed about the spot where the bark went down for a long time in the hope of finding others of the crew. The survivors were landed at Nassau November 11 and sent home by the Santiago, the first northbound steamer. The HALES was owned in New York. She was built at Newburyport, Massachusetts in 1877 and measured 834 tons.

Copyright 1879/1880/1881/1883/1884/1887/1889/1895/1913/1918 by The New York Times Company. Reprinted by permission.

NAME:	W.R. GRACE
RIG:	Ship
REGISTERED NUMBER:	80379
DATE & LOCATION BUILT:	1873; Bath, Maine by John McDonald
DATE SUNK:	September 10, 1889
REPORTED POSITION WHERE SUNK:	at point of Cape Henlopen 200 yards offshore
OWNER:	Benjamin Flint of New York; David Scriber; Kate Wallnut; Dudley Black of New York
MASTER AT TIME OF SINKING:	Captain Joseph Wallnut and 28 persons (all 29 saved)
CARGO AT TIME OF SINKING:	empty barrels (4/5's of these were salvaged)
HOME PORT:	New York City
LAST PORT SAILED FROM:	Havre, France
PORT BOUND FOR:	Philadelphia, Pennsylvania
WEATHER CONDITIONS AT TIME OF SINKING	heavy northeast storm
PHOTOGRAPH:	Courtesy W.R. Grace Company
CONSTRUCTION:	1,893 gross tons; 1,799 net tons; 3 decks; length 218.1'; breadth 42.8'; depth 20.8'; elliptic stern; gammen head

W.R. GRACE

NAME: WILLIAM H. SMITH

RIG: Schooner

REGISTERED NUMBER: 80370

DATE & LOCATION BUILT: 1873; Somerset County, Maryland

DATE SUNK: January 30, 1903

REPORTED POSITION WHERE SUNK: off coast of Delaware

MASTER AT TIME OF SINKING: 5 persons aboard (all 5 lost)

CARGO AT TIME OF SINKING: in ballast

HOME PORT: Newport News, Virginia

LAST PORT SAILED FROM: Hampton, Virginia

CONSTRUCTION: 27 tons gross; 26 tons net; length 55.2'; breadth 19.2'; depth 5.8'

NAME: WILLIAM O. SNOW

RIG: Schooner

DATE SUNK: left Norfolk September 5; September 12, 1889 by collision

REPORTED POSITION WHERE SUNK: 1-1/2 miles southeast of Brown Shoals, bayside of Delaware Breakwater

MASTER AT TIME OF SINKING: Captain Hatch and 8 crewmen; all rescued

HOME PORT: Taunton

LAST PORT SAILED FROM: Norfolk, Virginia

PORT BOUND FOR: Boston, Massachusetts

WEATHER CONDITIONS
AT TIME OF SINKING: hurricane

OTHER DATA:

New York Times
September 15, 1889

FALL RIVER, Mass. Sept. 14 - The steamer Saxon of the Windsor Line, from Philadelphia, arrived here this morning, twenty-four hours overdue. Besides a big cargo and her regular crew, she had on board the Captain and crew of the wrecked schooner WILLIAM O. SNOW of Taunton, reported to have been lost. The SNOW left Norfolk for Boston Sept. 5 with a cargo of coal. On the 10th she encountered the cyclone. To avoid the storm she put into Delaware Breakwater and anchored a mile and a half southeast of Brown Shoals, where it was expected she could ride out the hurricane. On Tuesday morning she met with a mishap which sent her to the bottom. The tug C.W. Morse, with coal barges in tow, put into the Breakwater and anchored near the SNOW. On Monday night one of the barges broke away and early Tuesday morning there was a tremendous crash.

The barge, carried along by the gale, struck the schooner full on. The latter filled, went over on her beam ends, and disappeared. Her Captain and crew took to the rigging and hung on for dear life. The barge went down soon after the collision, and her crew, it is feared, went with her. Her name is unknown. Lashed to the spars and crosstrees, Capt. Hatch and his eight men remained forty-eight hours, with the seas constantly breaking over them. Just as hope was abandoned, the Saxon, attempting to make her way out, saw the crew. Volunteers were called for, and four brave men undertook the rescue in a small boat. It was a perilous task, and time and again it looked as if all hands would be lost. They persevered, however, and succeeded in taking off the nine men. Copyright 1879/1880/1881/1883/1884/1887/1889/1895/1913/1918 by The New York Times Company. Reprinted by permission.

NAME:	ZELINDA
RIG:	Bark
DATE SUNK:	July 10, 1864
REPORTED POSITION WHERE SUNK:	35 miles off Maryland coast 37° 33'N; 74° 20'W
OWNER:	Union Navy
CARGO AT TIME OF SINKING:	ballast
HOME PORT:	Eastport, Maine
LAST PORT SAILED FROM:	Matanzas
PORT BOUND FOR:	Philadelphia, Pennsylvania
CONSTRUCTION:	559 tons
OTHER DATA:	burned by C.S.S. Florida

LIST OF SOURCES

The New York Times
The Philadelphia Public Ledger
Maryland Gazette
The Baltimore Sunpapers
National Oceanic and Atmospheric Administration
Mrs. Jean Haviland, Baltimore, Maryland
Public Record Office, KEW Richmond, Surrey, England
United States Coast Guard
United States Navy Ships History Division
National Archives
Mariners Museum of Newport News, Virginia
Enoch Pratt Free Library, Baltimore, Maryland
Maine Maritime Museum Bath, Maine
Steamship Historical Society of the United States, Baltimore, Maryland
Zwaanendael Museum, Lewes, Delaware
United States Life Saving Service Records 1876-1914
United States Merchant Ship Losses, December 7, 1941 to August 14, 1945
John Lochhead - wreck list from 1841 to 1846
Lloyd's Register
The National Watercraft Collection
Merchant Vessels of the United States, United States Coast Guard
Shipwrecks off the New Jersey Coast, Walter and Richard Krotee
Encyclopedia of American Shipwrecks, Bruce D. Berman
Hang and Obstructions to Trawl Fishing, Atlantic Coast of United States, University of North Carolina, Sea Grant Publication
Guide to Sunken Ships in American Waters, A.A.L. Lonsdale and H.R. Kaplan
Navy Wreck List, 1957, United States Navy Hydrographic Office
Wreck Information List, March 10, 1945, United States Hydrographic Office
Great Gales and Dire Disasters, E.R. Snow
Marine Salvage Operations, Edward M. Brady
Sinkings, Salvages, and Shipwrecks, Robert F. Burgess
History of American Sailing Ships, Howard I. Chapelle
Merchant Sail Volumes 1 through 6, William A. Fairburn
Primer of Shipwreck Research and Records for Skindivers, including an informal bibliography listing over 300 sources of shipwreck information, Robert A. Fleming
Steamboat Disasters and Railroad Accidents in the United States, S.A. Howland
Merchant Steam Vessels of the United States, 1807-1868, William M. Lytle
Great Coal Schooners of New England, 1870-1909, J. Lewis Parker
United States Revenue Cutter Service Annual Reports, 1912-1913, Government Printing Office
Great Ship Disasters, Adolf A. Hoehling
Pilots of The Bay and River Delaware, James E. Marvil, M.D.

www.ingramcontent.com/pod-product-compliance
Lightning Source LLC
Chambersburg PA
CBHW070728160426
43192CB00009B/1353